JUMP AT HOME
GRADE
2

ALSO BY JOHN MIGHTON

The Myth of Ability

The End of Ignorance

JUMP MATH SERIES

JUMP at Home Grade 1

JUMP at Home Grade 2

JUMP at Home Grade 3

JUMP at Home Grade 4

JUMP at Home Grade 5

JUMP at Home Grade 6

JUMP at Home Grade 7

JUMP at Home Grade 8

Worksheets for the JUMP Math Program

JOHN MIGHTON

ANANSI

This edition published in 2010 by
House of Anansi Press Inc.
www.houseofanansi.com

House of Anansi Press is committed to protecting our natural environment. As part of our efforts, the interior of this book is printed on Ancient Forest Friendly paper that contains 100% recycled fibres (40% post-consumer waste and 60% pre-consumer waste) and is processed chlorine-free.

Some of the material in this book has previously been published by JUMP Math.

Every reasonable effort has been made to contact the holders of copyright for materials reproduced in this work. The publishers will gladly receive information that will enable them to rectify any inadvertent errors or omissions in subsequent editions.

20 19 18 17 16   5 6 7 8 9

Library and Archives Canada Cataloguing in Publication

Cataloguing data available from Library and Archives Canada

Library of Congress Control Number: 2010924087

Acknowledgements
Writers: Dr. John Mighton, Dr. Sindi Sabourin, and Dr. Anna Klebanov
Text design: Pam Lostracco
Layout: Rita Camacho, Pam Lostracco, and Ilyana Martinez
Illustrations: Pam Lostracco

This book, like the JUMP program itself, is made possible by the efforts of the volunteers and staff of JUMP Math.

We acknowledge for their financial support of our publishing program the Canada Council for the Arts, the Ontario Arts Council, and the Government of Canada through the Canada Book Fund.

Printed and bound in Canada

Contents

Unit 1: Number Sense 1

Unit 2: Patterns and Algebra 1

Unit 3: Measurement 1

Unit 4: Probability and Data Management 1

Unit 5: Number Sense 2

Unit 6: Patterns and Algebra 2

Unit 7: Measurement 2

Introduction: **About JUMP Math**

There is a prevalent myth in our society that people are born with mathematical talent, and others simply do not have the ability to succeed. Recent discoveries in cognitive science are challenging this myth of ability. The brain is not hard-wired, but continues to change and develop throughout life. Steady, incremental learning can result in the emergence of new abilities.

The carefully designed mathematics in the JUMP Math program provide the necessary skills and knowledge to give your child the joy of success in mathematics. Through step-by-step learning, students celebrate success with every question, thereby increasing achievement and reducing math anxiety.

John Mighton: **Founder of JUMP Math**

"Nine years ago I was looking for a way to give something back to my local community. It occurred to me that I should try to help kids who needed help with math. Mathematicians don't always make the best teachers because mathematics has become obvious to them; they can have trouble seeing why their students are having trouble. But because I had struggled with math myself, I wasn't inclined to blame my students if they couldn't move forward."
— John Mighton, *The End of Ignorance*

JUMP Math, a national charity dedicated to improving mathematical literacy, was founded by John Mighton, a mathematician, bestselling author, and award-winning playwright. The organization grew out of John's work with a core group of volunteers in a "tutoring club"; their goal was to meet the needs of the most challenged students from local schools. Over the next three years John developed the early material — simple handouts for the tutors to use during their one-on-one teaching sessions with individual students. This period was one of experimentation in developing the JUMP Math method. Eventually, John began to work in local inner-city schools, by placing tutors in the classrooms. This led to the next period of innovation: using the JUMP Math method on small groups of students.

Teachers responded enthusiastically to the success they saw in their students and wanted to adapt the method for classroom use. In response, the needs of the teachers for curriculum-based resources were met by the development of workbooks. These started out as a series of three remedial books with limited accompanying teacher materials, released in fall 2003. The effectiveness of these workbooks led quickly to the development of grade-specific, curriculum-based workbooks. The grade-specific books were first released in 2004. Around that time, the power of teacher networks in creating learning communities was beginning to take shape.

Inspired by the work he has done with thousands of students over the past twenty years, John has systematically developed an approach to teaching mathematics that is based on fostering brain plasticity and emergent intelligence, and on the idea that children have more potential in mathematics than is generally believed. Linking new research in cognitive science to his extensive observations of students, John calls for a re-examination of the assumptions that underlie current methods of teaching mathematics.

JUMP Math, as a program and as an organization, developed in response to the needs of the students, teachers, schools, and communities where John and the volunteers were working. Recognizing the potential of all students to succeed in mathematics, and to succeed in school, was the motivation that John needed to dedicate more than ten years of his life developing a mathematics program that achieved his vision.

JUMP Math: **An Innovative Approach**

In only ten years, JUMP Math has gone from John's kitchen table to a thriving organization reaching more than 50,000 students with high-quality learning resources and training for 2,000 teachers. It continues to work with community organizations to reach struggling students through homework clubs and after-school programs. Through the generous support of our sponsors, JUMP Math donates resources to classrooms and homework clubs across Canada. The organization has also inspired thousands of community volunteers and teachers to donate their time as tutors, mentors, and trainers.

JUMP Math is unique; it builds on the belief that every child can be successful at mathematics by
- Promoting positive learning environments and building confidence through praise and encouragement;
- Maintaining a balanced approach to mathematics by concurrently addressing conceptual and procedural learning;
- Achieving understanding and mastery by breaking mathematics down into small sequential steps;
- Keeping all students engaged and attentive by "raising the bar" incrementally; and,
- Guiding students strategically to explore and discover the beauty of mathematics.

JUMP Math recognizes the importance of reducing math anxiety. Research in psychology has shown that our brains are extremely fallible: our working memories are poor, we are easily overwhelmed by too much new information, and we require a good deal of practice to consolidate skills and concepts. These mental challenges are compounded when we are anxious. The JUMP approach has been shown to reduce math anxiety significantly.

JUMP Math scaffolds mathematical concepts rigorously and completely. The materials were designed by a team of mathematicians and educators who have a deep understanding of and a love for mathematics. Concepts are introduced in rigorous steps, and prerequisite skills are included in the lesson. Breaking down concepts and skills into steps is often necessary even with the more able students. Math is a subject in which a gifted student can become a struggling student almost overnight, because mathematical knowledge is cumulative.

Consistent with emerging brain research, JUMP Math provides materials and methods that minimize differences between students, allowing teachers, tutors, and parents to more effectively improve student performance in mathematics. Today, parents have access to this unique innovation in mathematics learning with the revised JUMP at Home books.

JUMP Math at Home

JUMP at Home has been developed by mathematicians and educators to complement the mathematics curriculum that your child learns at school. Each grade covers core skills and knowledge to help your child succeed in mathematics. The program focuses on building number sense, pattern recognition, and foundations for algebra.

JUMP at Home is designed to boost every student's confidence, skills, and knowledge. Struggling students will benefit from practice in small steps, while good students will be provided with new ways to understand concepts that will help them enjoy mathematics even more and to exceed their own expectations.

JUMP Math in Schools

JUMP Math also publishes full curriculum-based resources — including student workbooks, teacher guides with daily lesson plans, and blackline masters — that cover all of the Ontario and the Western Canada mathematics curriculum. For more information, please visit the JUMP Math website, www.jumpmath.org, to find out how to order.

Evidence that JUMP Math Works

JUMP Math is a leader in promoting third-party research about its work. A recent study by researchers at the Ontario Institute for Studies in Education (OISE), the University of Toronto, and Simon Fraser University found that in JUMP Math classrooms conceptual understanding improved significantly for weaker students. In Lambeth, England, researchers reported that after using JUMP Math for one year, 69 percent of students who were two years behind were assessed at grade level.

Cognitive scientists from The Hospital for Sick Children in Toronto recently conducted a randomized-controlled study of the effectiveness of the JUMP math program. Studies of such scientific rigour remain relatively rare in mathematics education research in North America. The results showed that students who received JUMP instruction outperformed students who received the methods of instruction their teachers would normally use, on well-established measures of math achievement.

Using JUMP at Home

"In the twenty years that I have been teaching mathematics to children, I have never met an educator who would say that students who lack confidence in their intellectual or academic abilities are likely to do well in school. JUMP Math has been carefully designed to boost confidence. It has proven to be an extremely effective approach for convincing even the most challenged student that they can do well in mathematics." — John Mighton

Helping your child discover the joy of mathematics can be fun and productive. You are not the teacher but the tutor. When having fun with mathematics, remember the JUMP Math T.U.T.O.R. principles:

Take responsibility for learning:
If your child doesn't understand a concept, it can always be clarified further or explained differently. As the adult, you are responsible for helping your child understand. If they don't get it, don't get frustrated — get creative!

Use positive reinforcement:
Children like to be rewarded when they succeed. Praise and encouragement build excitement and foster an appetite for learning. The more confidence a student has, the more likely they are to be engaged.

Take small steps:
In mathematics, it is always possible to make something easier. Always use the JUMP Math worksheets to break down the question into a series of small steps. Practice, practice, practice!

Only indicate correct answers:
Your child's confidence can be shaken by a lack of success. Place checkmarks for correct answers, then revisit questions that your child is having difficulty with. Never use Xs!

Raise the bar:
When your child has mastered a particular concept, challenge them by posing a question that is slightly more difficult. As your child meets these small challenges, you will see their focus and excitement increase.

And remember: if your child is falling behind, teach the number facts! It is a serious mistake to think that students who don't know their number facts can always get by in mathematics using a calculator or other aids. Students can certainly perform operations on a calculator, but they cannot begin to solve problems if they lack a sense of numbers. Students need to be able to see patterns in numbers, and to make estimates and predictions about numbers, in order to have any success in mathematics. We have put together some fun activities to help you and your child get ready for mathematics!

Counting Backwards

In mathematics, it is important for your child to learn how to count backwards. Many children find counting backwards much more difficult than counting forwards. Here are some things you can do to help your child learn and practice this skill.

Keep Score . . . Backwards!

Count backwards every time you make a catch or hit a ball when you play games such as ping-pong or catch. Start at 5, 10, or 20, and play until you reach 0. Did someone drop or miss the ball? Don't start counting back from the last number — add 3 first! For example, if someone misses the ball at 11, start counting back again from 14. (Your child knows how to add 3, so let him/her do it!)

Count Down the Time

Next time you use a timer around the house (e.g., to microwave popcorn), tell your child how you know when the time is almost up. Watch and chant the last 10 or 20 seconds of the countdown together.

Play Plus or Minus 1

(Game adapted from *Card Games for Smart Kids* by Dr. Margie Golick.)

You will need one deck of cards. Start by removing all of the face cards (King, Queen, Jack) from the deck.

Goal: To place all 40 cards into a new pile

To play:

1. Put the deck face down and turn over the top card. What number is it? Start a new pile with this card.
2. Turn over the next card. What number is it? If it is **1 more or 1 less** than the last card, add it to the pile. Otherwise, put it in another pile (the discard pile).
3. Keep turning cards over and putting them in the appropriate piles until the deck runs out. Then repeat with the cards in the discard pile (and start a new discard pile).
4. Keep playing with the cards in the discard pile. Eventually, you will have placed all the cards into the new pile (and you win!) or you will have some cards left over.

Variation:

Play Plus or Minus 2: Cards go into the new pile if they are **2 more or 2 less** than the last card drawn.

Wait or Go?

Some pedestrian traffic signals include a countdown. If you see such a signal, point out to your child when the countdown starts. Have your child watch the countdown and count backwards with it. Discuss how the countdown helps pedestrians cross the street safely. How do the lights change when the number reaches 0? How does knowing that 9 is far from 0, but 2 is close to 0 help you decide if you have enough time to cross the street or if you should wait?

Sorting

In mathematics, it is important for your child to learn how to sort things into groups. Here are some things you can do together to help your child practice sorting.

Sort laundry

Ask your child to help you sort the laundry into different groups, such as

- shirts, pants, socks
- dark clothes, light clothes
- your clothes, my clothes

Discuss with your child how all of the items in a group are the same and how the groups differ. Can your child think of another way to sort the laundry?

Sort Grocery Items

Ask your child to help you sort grocery items into groups, such as

- dairy products, meat products, other
- things we store in the fridge, things we don't store in the fridge
- things we eat, things we don't eat (e.g., tissues, cat litter, soap)

You can also sort by shape or colour. Can your child think of another way to sort the items?

Sort Cutlery

Ask your child to sort cutlery before putting it away. What groups did your child create? Ask your child to explain why he/she sorted the items that way.

Sort Toys, Books, and Games

Ask your child to sort toys, books, and games before putting them away. If your child's toys are already sorted (e.g., books in a bookcase, games in a box), ask your child to describe how they are sorted. Which items are grouped together? How many groups are there?

How Are Items Sorted?

Look for examples of sorting everywhere you go: at the grocery store, in the library, in stores and shops. Discuss how the items on a shelf or in an aisle are sorted and why they might be sorted that way. For example,

- shoes in a shoe store are often sorted first by age and gender (men, women, kids) and then by type (dress shoes, running shoes, boots, and so on);
- flowers in a flower shop are sorted by type (carnations, lilies, roses) and then sometimes by colour; and
- books at the library or in a bookstore are sorted by subject and by age (fiction, cookbooks, children's books, and so on).

Length

In mathematics, your child needs to learn about length. Comparing lengths is something we all do in daily life. Here are some ways you can compare lengths together at home.

Compare Lengths Directly — Socks

Ask your child to help you sort and match socks after washing. Demonstrate comparing two socks of different lengths by lining up the heel-to-toe parts side by side. Ask: Which one is longer? Which one do you think is mine? Sort the remaining socks into two piles, long and short. (This activity will work best if you have many pairs of plain, unpatterned socks or at least two different sizes of the same pattern.) You can finish sorting and matching the socks together. Once you have sorted them by size, match them by colour and pattern.

Compare Lengths Directly and Indirectly — Hands and Feet

Ask your child: Whose hand is bigger — yours or mine? How can we check? Hold your hand up to your child's to compare them. Then compare the length of your hands to the length of your mittens or gloves. Ask: Will my hand fit in your mitten? Will your hand fit in mine? Repeat for feet and socks/shoes.

Now ask: What's longer — your foot or my hand? How can we check? Before comparing them directly, compare your child's shoe or sock to your glove. Ask: Which one is longer? Your child might want to revise his/her answer to the first question. Now line your hand up with your child's foot to compare the lengths directly.

Here's another way to compare the lengths of your hands and feet indirectly: Trace your child's foot onto paper and ask your child to trace your hand onto paper. Cut the two tracings out and place them one on top of the other.

Compare and Order Lengths

Ask relatives or friends who live far away to trace one hand or paint a handprint onto paper and mail it to you. Compare their hands to yours and your child's. Order the hands from longest to shortest. Who has the longest hand? Who has the shortest hand? With older children, use a ruler and measure directly.

Basic Operations

In mathematics, your child needs to know addition, subtraction, and skip counting forwards (e.g., 5, 10, 15, . . .) and backwards (e.g., 10, 8, 6, . . .). If you have stairs in your home, the games below can help your child master these concepts.

To begin, attach numbers to each step, starting with 1 on the first (bottom) step and going up. (Higher numbers are thus higher in space.) Put a 0 on the floor before the first step. You will also need dice for each game.

Games for 1 Player

- **Adding on Stairs.** Model finding 5 + 3: Stand on the step marked 5 and go up 3 steps. Give children a die to roll. If the first roll is 5, they move up 5 steps and say 0 + 5 = 5. If the second roll is 4, they move up 4 steps and say 5 + 4 = 9. Play continues until children reach the top of the stairs. At the end, children will have to roll the exact number needed to land on the top step.
- **Subtracting on Stairs.** Play as above, but start on the top step and move down, e.g., 8 − 3 = 5.
- **Skip Counting by 2s on Stairs.** Children walk up the steps, one at a time, and say every number that their left (or right) foot lands on. Children should start at 0, and take the number of steps determined by the roll of a die. If they roll a 5, they take 5 steps and say either "1, 3, 5" or "0, 2, 4." The goal is to get to the top of the stairs.
- **Skip Counting Back by 2s on Stairs.** Play as above, but start at the top step and move down.

A Cooperative Game for 2–4 Players

This game combines addition and subtraction. Note that players do not play against each other, but instead work as a team. Parents and children can play together.

- **Adding or Subtracting on Stairs.** Players start on predetermined steps (e.g., 0, 5, 10, and 20). Each player rolls the die in turn and moves accordingly. Players can choose whether to move up (add) or down (subtract), but there can never be more than one player on a step at any time, and players cannot move to the bottom (1) or top step once play has begun. Players say the addition or subtraction sentence corresponding to their move (e.g., 8 − 2 = 6) and try to make as many moves as possible as a team before they get stuck. Play again and try to improve. A supervising or participating adult (or older child) can keep track of how many moves were made.

Telling the Time

In mathematics, your child is learning how to tell time. Your child knows that the "short hand" on a clock is called the hour hand. Because it is longer than the hour hand, we call the minute hand "the long hand."

In class, children often talk about what they do when the hour hand is pointing at different numbers. For example; when the hour hand points at the 10, we go outside for recess. When the hour hand points at the 3, we know that school is almost over.

Here are some ways you can talk about time at home. You will need an analogue clock (a clock with hands).

What Would You Be Doing If . . .

At different times on the weekend, ask your child what he or she would be doing if this were a school day. Emphasize the position of the hour hand each time.

Where Is the Short Hand? What Will We Do?

Ask your child where the short hand is pointing at different times during the day, such as at mealtimes or other regularly scheduled activities (e.g., lessons, visits to friends or family). Then do the reverse: Point out the position of the short hand and ask your child to identify the activity. If you eat supper around 6 p.m., you might say: The short hand is close to the 6. What will we be doing soon?

It's Time For . . .

Identify events that happen at the same time every day or week. For example, if your child has a favourite television show, point out where the short hand is when the show starts. Ask: Is the show on at the same time every day? Every Saturday? How could we check? (Check that channel every day at the same time for a week and record the answers in a chart.)

Changes in Time

Investigate natural events that change predictably over time. Record the times of the events daily or weekly for a few weeks (or more!). Then look for patterns. For example:

- What time does it get dark outside?

- How do shadows change? Find a landmark or familiar object near your home that is sometimes in the shade and sometimes in the light. What time does it come into or out of the shade?

"Children will never fulfill their extraordinary potential until we remember how it felt to have so much potential ourselves. There was nothing we weren't inspired to look at or hold, or that we weren't determined to find out how to do. Open the door to the world of mathematics so your child can pass through." — John Mighton

Games, Activities, and Puzzles:
Notes on Games, Activities, and Puzzles

Make your own Mindsweeper game.

For this game, you will need a copy of the activity page *Blank Mindsweeper Grids* on page xxiii. To prepare to play "Mindsweeper," start by filling in four stars in the blank 4 x 4 grid, or five stars in the blank 5 x 5 grid. You may arrange the stars in any way you want. Then, in each non-starred square, write the number of starred squares that it is touching. Two examples, with a 4 x 4 grid filled in, are shown below.

2	*	3	1
2	*	3	*
1	1	3	2
0	0	1	*

2	*	2	*
*	3	3	2
2	3	*	1
*	2	1	1

Cover the squares on the grid with coins about the size of a penny. To play the game, the player removes coins from the squares one at a time. The player may decide to stop removing coins at any time. The player then counts how many starred squares are still covered by coins and how many numbered squares remain covered. The player wins if there are more starred squares still covered than numbered squares covered.

Note: This game is slightly different than the traditional form of the Minesweeper video game. In the traditional game, the player tries to remove all the pennies from the numbered squares, but loses if he or she uncovers any starred square. The Mindsweeper grids can also be used to play the traditional game.

Ordering Number Words

Give your child index cards with number words on them and have your child organize them in order.

Food Sale

Use the activity page *Food Sale.* You or your child could cut out the receipts. You can take turns being the cashier and the customer. The cashier writes out the receipts for the customer. Each customer is given 5 dimes and should buy as much as they can for their 50¢.

Variation: Try to buy a balanced meal for 50¢, one item from each of the four food groups.

Extension: Use a calculator to add the total amount of money spent, and subtract it from 50¢. Is this the amount of money you have left? Discuss whether you could have paid for all the items at the same time instead of separately.

Adding and Subtracting on Stairs

Play the games Adding on Stairs and Subtracting on Stairs and Adding or Subtracting on Stairs (see JUMP At Home — Introduction for a description of these games). Then have your child do the activities *Adding on Stairs* and *Subtracting on Stairs*.

Reading Number Words on Cheques

On the website **http://www.funbrain.com/numwords/index.html** your child can use Method 2 and write the digit in the correct place on the cheque. The number word is written on the cheque. No money notation is used. Be sure your child notices that on the top-left corner of the screen, the computer will tell them if they are correct.

Writing Number Words on Cheques

On the website **http://www.funbrain.com/numwords/index.html** your child can use Method 1 and write the number word in the correct place on the cheque. The corresponding digit from 1–10 is written on the cheque.

Adding Number Words

a) one + one = _____ _____ _____

b) three + four = _____ _____ _____ _____ _____

c) seven – one = _____ _____ _____

d) _____ _____ _____ + _____ _____ _____ _____ _____ = _____ _____ _____

    (there are several solutions; have your child find as many as they can)

e) _____ _____ _____ _____ + _____ _____ _____ = _____ _____ _____ _____ _____ _____

    (five + six = eleven or nine + two = eleven)

Completing sentences

Encourage your child to write the numbers above the number words.

a) Seven is _____ more than three.

b) Rita is seven years old. Matias is three years old. Rita is _____ years older than Matias.

c) _____ is six more than three.

Word search puzzle

Find, horizontally, vertically or diagonally:
one, ten, eleven, two, twenty, twelve, three, thirty, four, forty, seventeen, fifty, zero, eight

W	T	I	T	W	E	N	T	Y
N	W	T	E	O	E	R	T	S
F	O	U	R	V	N	Y	W	P
S	E	V	E	N	T	E	E	N
Z	T	L	E	R	R	I	L	F
E	E	F	I	F	T	Y	V	O
R	N	H	G	N	G	A	E	R
O	T	T	H	R	E	E	N	T
D	S	U	T	M	M	E	R	Y

Use the leftover letters to finish the message.

The four seasons are: fall, __ __ __ __ __ __,

__ __ __ __ __ __, __ __ __ __ __ __ __ __ __.

(This was made using the puzzle-making tool at
http://www.superkids.com/aweb/tools/words/serach)

Crossword puzzle

You could use an online puzzle-making tool to create crossword puzzles, for example, **http://www.puzzle-maker.com/CW/**. Since your child may not know how to spell the words, you should make the list of number words available for reference, including the words for tens (ten, twenty, thirty, and so on) and the words for zero to twelve. You could use clues such as "one + thirty" or "twenty + twenty" or "fifty − four" and so on.

Logic — First out or last out

If you have access to the stacking rings toy, demonstrate putting the first one in, then the second, and then the third. Then take them out, one at a time. Ask your child: Was the largest one the first one in or the last one in? Was it the first one out or last one out? Was the first one in the first one out or the last one out? (The first one in is the last one out.) Discuss whether the first one in is the first or last out in other circumstances:

- a line-up for tickets
- a Kleenex box
- a line-up for a slide
- a funnel
- a stack of pancakes

If possible, have some of these items on hand. Then discuss situations where you cannot tell whether the first one in will be the first or last out. Examples: an elevator, a plate of cookies.

Hundreds Chart Puzzles

1. Give your child partially completed rows and columns of a hundreds chart and have them fill in the missing numbers:

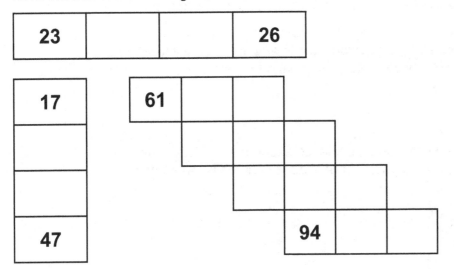

Then have your child cut out the pieces and glue them onto the activity page *Hundreds Chart* as a way to check their answers.

2. Give your child the activity page *Hundreds Chart Puzzles.*

2-Attribute patterns in music

Have your child extend the pattern.

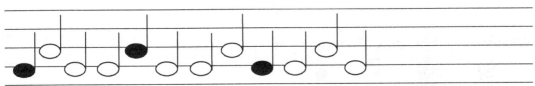

Fractions of apples or oranges

Bring out some apples or oranges. Cut some in half and some in fourths and some in eighths. Ask your child to decide which is more between different fractions: for example, one half or three eighths. Encourage them to put three eighths together so that they can see that it is not quite half.

Time

1. Have your child search through magazines to find watches, clocks, timers, etc. They can create a collage of everything they cut out and make up a title for their collage. Those who are ready to read the time could write what time is shown underneath the cut-out clocks.

2. Online activity for your child to fill in the missing numbers on the clock face.
   http://www.learningplanet.com/act/tw/index.asp?contentid=410

3. Ask your child to create a timeline starting at 7 a.m., and ending at 7 p.m. and to draw and write about what they are doing at each hour. Then ask them to generate a list of activities they do that take about an hour.

4. Ask your child to create a timeline starting at 7:00 a.m. and ending at 8:30 p.m. and to draw and write about what they are doing at each half hour. Then ask them to generate a list of activities they do that each take about a half hour.

5. Time your child to see how many of each activity from *How Long is a Minute?* they can do in a minute. Point out that a minute is the amount of time it takes the second hand (the fast hand) to move all the way around the clock.

Hanji puzzles

Your child can add in two ways by counting the shaded squares first in each row and then in each column. Note that the total number of shaded squares is the same no matter how they are counted!

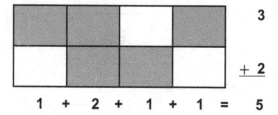

3

+ 2

1 + 2 + 1 + 1 = 5

Hanji puzzles ask your child to do the reverse — given the number of shaded squares in each row and column, determine which squares are shaded. The 3-page activity *Hanji Puzzles* guides your child in a step-by-step approach to be able to solve simple Hanji puzzles.

Multiplication

1. Have your child use this 6 by 6 array of dots to multiply.

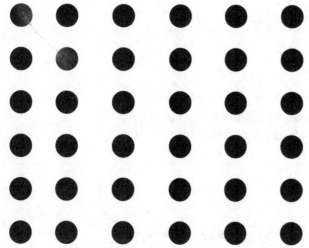

Use two sheets of paper to cover up part of the grid to multiply. For example, to multiply 2 × 3, cover up all but the first two rows and cover all but the first three columns:

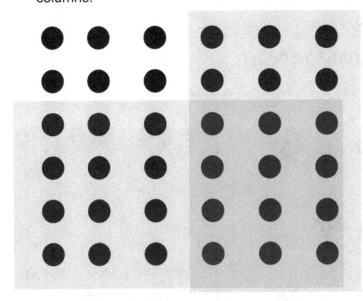

This leaves two rows of three, which leaves 3 + 3 = 6 dots or 2 × 3 = 6 dots.

2. Have your child fill in the blanks with the correct symbol (+, −, ×, ÷):

5 [ ] 3 = 2

5 [ ] 5 = 10

5 [ ] 3 = 15

5 [ ] 5 = 25

5 [ ] 3 = 8

5 [ ] 5 = 0

Roman Numbers

Look at the Roman playing cards.
Translate the numbers from Roman to English.

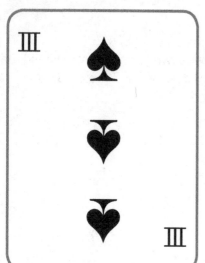

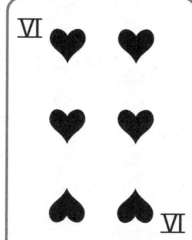

III = _____

V = _____

IV = _____

VII = _____

VI = _____

II = _____

Blank Mindsweeper Grids

Mindsweeper

Mindsweeper

No unauthorized copying

Counting Starred Squares

Colour the squares touching the bold square.

 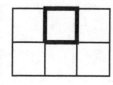 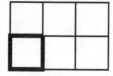 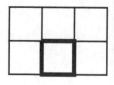

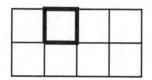 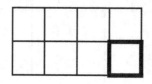 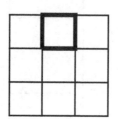 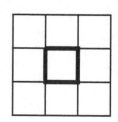

How many starred squares is the bold square touching?

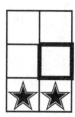 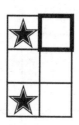 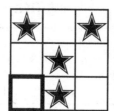 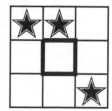

In each square, write how many starred squares it is touching.

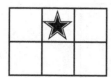   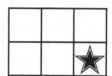

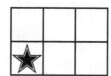 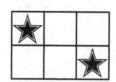 

Counting Starred Squares *(continued)*

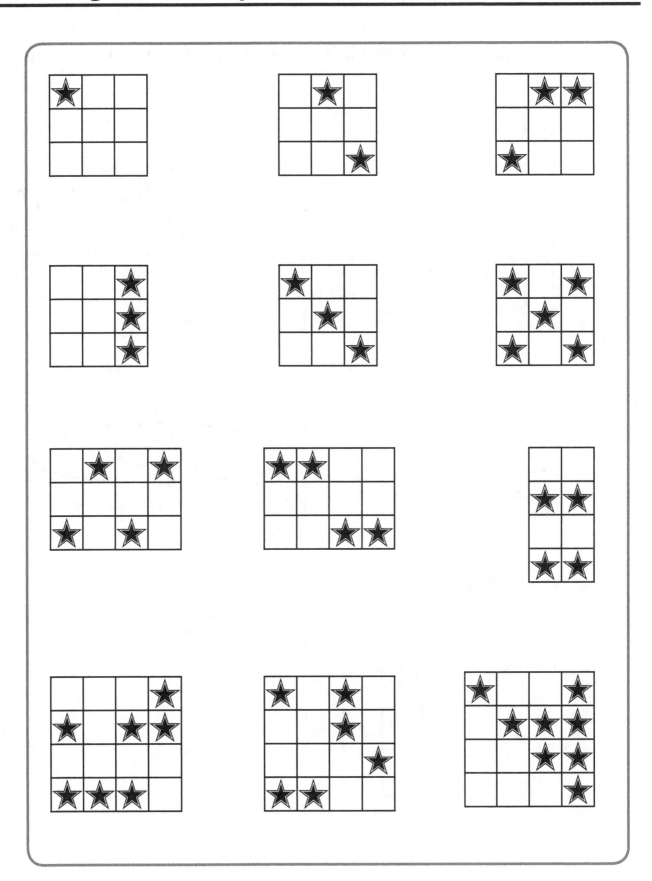

First or Last Out

Decide if the first (1st) one in will be the **first out**, the **last out**, or if **you can't tell.**

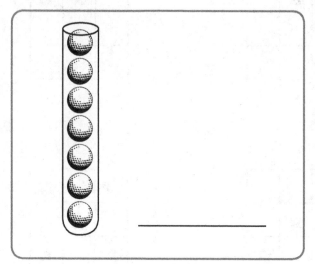

_____

_____

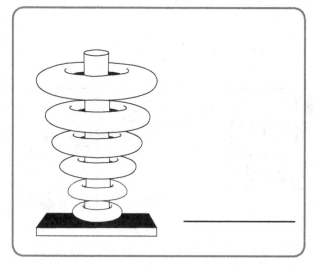

_____

_____

_____

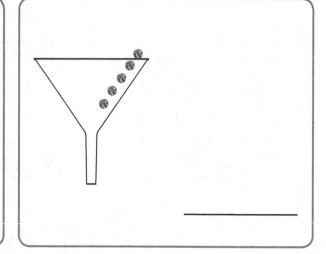

_____

Number Word Search

Word Search:

~~zero~~	one	two	three
four	five	six	seven
eight	nine	ten	

t	z	e	r	o	t	f
s	e	v	e	n	h	o
i	i	h	e	e	r	u
x	g	f	n	i	e	r
t	h	f	i	v	e	r
w	t	e	n	e	f	i
o	g	h	e	t	e	r

Use the extra letters. Who protects the neighbourhood?

___ ___ ___ ___   ___ ___ ___ ___ - ___ ___ ___ ___ ___ ___ ___

Adding on Stairs

Liam goes up 3 steps. Where does he end up?

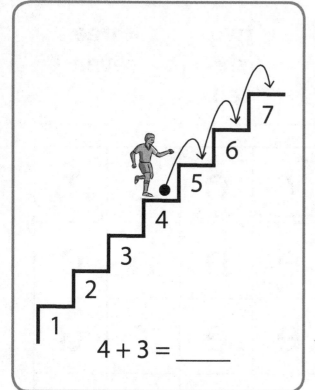

$4 + 3 =$ _____

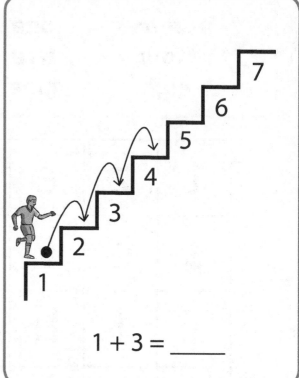

$1 + 3 =$ _____

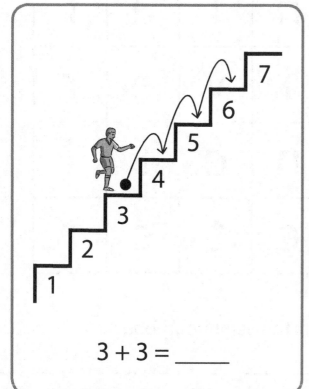

$3 + 3 =$ _____

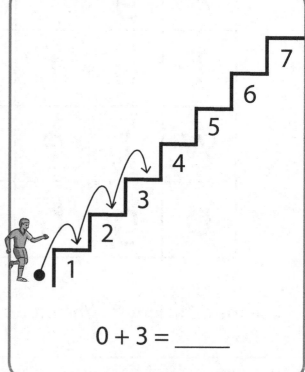

$0 + 3 =$ _____

Adding on Stairs *(continued)*

Count the steps.

Fill in the blanks.

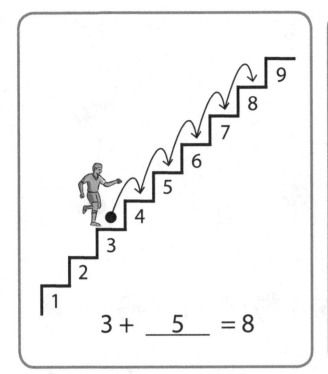

$$3 + \underline{\quad 5 \quad} = 8$$

$$5 + \underline{\qquad} = 9$$

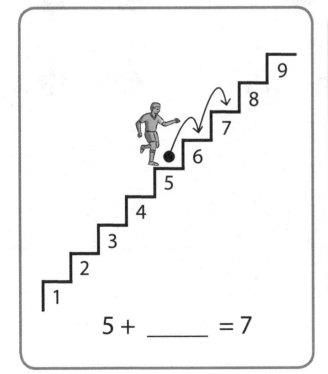

$$5 + \underline{\qquad} = 7$$

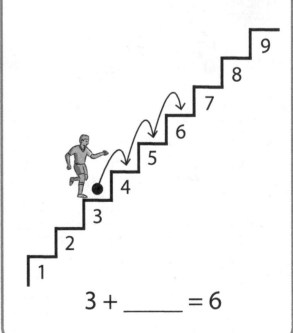

$$3 + \underline{\qquad} = 6$$

Roman Numbers Addition Page

Look at the Roman playing cards.

Add in Roman.

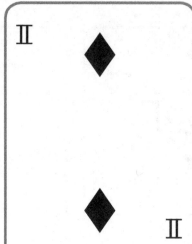

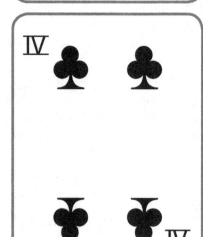

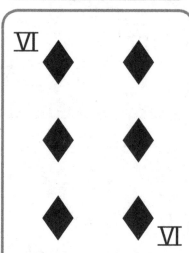

I + III = _____

II + IV = _____

III + II = _____

V + I = _____

Modelling Subtraction

Subtract.

a)  A B C D F $5 - 3 = \underline{\quad}$

b) 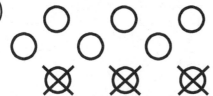 $9 - 3 = \underline{\quad}$

c)  $7 - 4 = \underline{\quad}$

d)  $9 - 2 = \underline{\quad}$

e)  $4 - 1 = \underline{\quad}$

f) 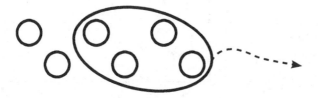 $6 - 4 = \underline{\quad}$

g) 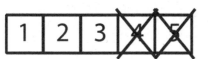 $5 - 2 = \underline{\quad}$

Models of Counting Back

Subtract.

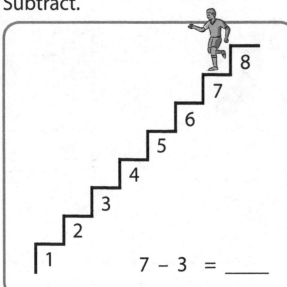

7 – 3 = _____

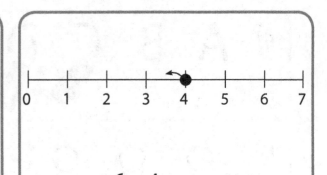

6 – 4 = _____

9

_____	_____
9 – 1	9 – 2

9 – 2 = _____

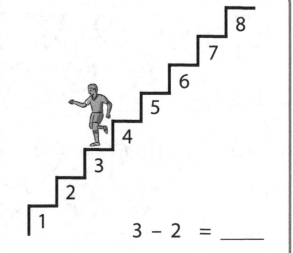

3 – 2 = _____

4 – 3 = _____

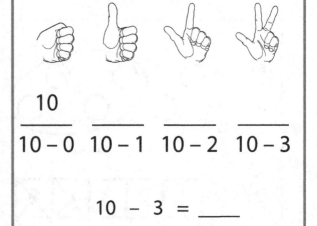

10

_____	_____	_____	_____
10 – 0	10 – 1	10 – 2	10 – 3

10 – 3 = _____

Models of Counting On

Subtract.

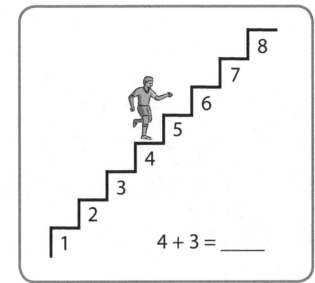

4 + 3 = _____

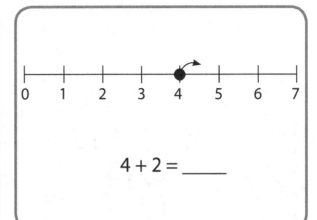

4 + 2 = _____

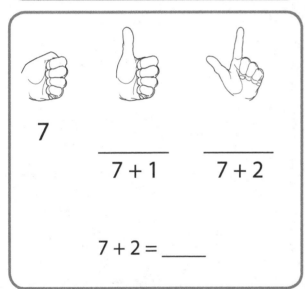

7 + 2 = _____

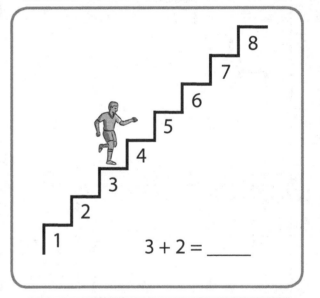

3 + 2 = _____

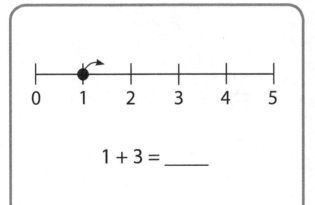

1 + 3 = _____

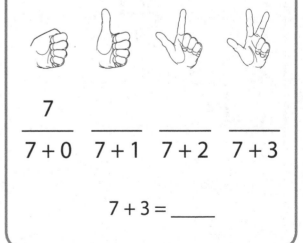

7 + 3 = _____

Subtracting on Stairs

Liam goes down 3 steps. Where does he end up?

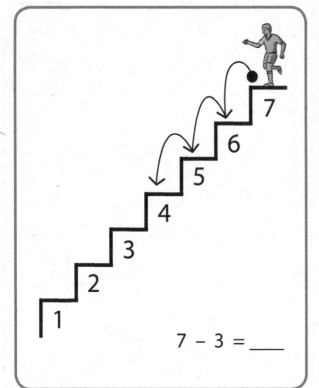

7 − 3 = ___

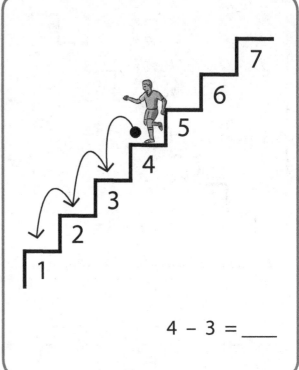

4 − 3 = ___

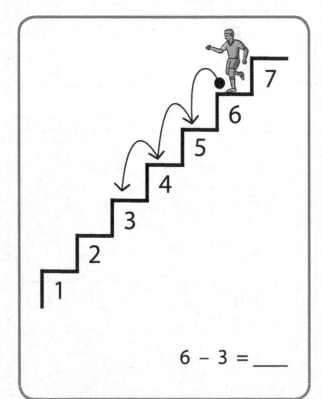

6 − 3 = ___

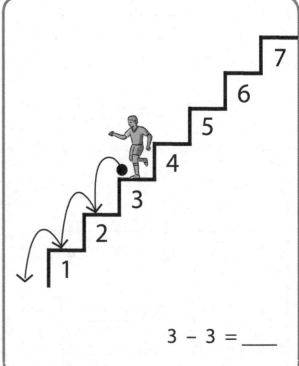

3 − 3 = ___

Subtracting on Stairs *(continued)*

Count the steps.

Fill in the blanks.

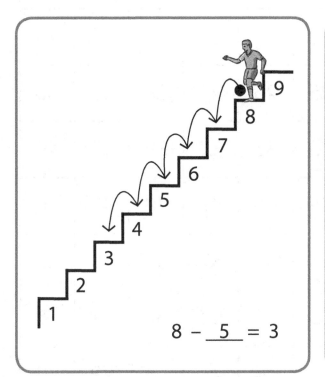

8 – _5_ = 3

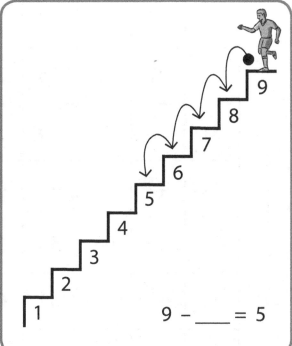

9 – ___ = 5

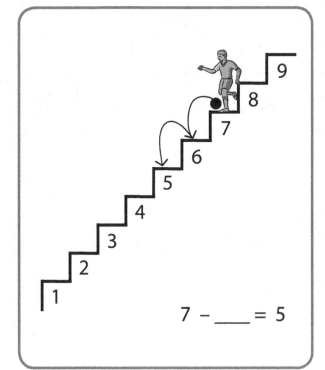

7 – ___ = 5

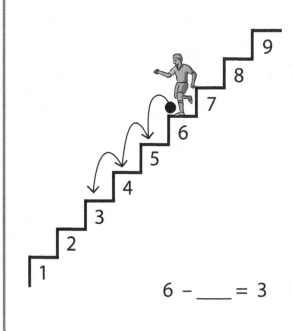

6 – ___ = 3

Full Hundreds Chart

1	2	3	4	5	6	7	8	9	10
11	12	13	14	15	16	17	18	19	20
21	22	23	24	25	26	27	28	29	30
31	32	33	34	35	36	37	38	39	40
41	42	43	44	45	46	47	48	49	50
51	52	53	54	55	56	57	58	59	60
61	62	63	64	65	66	67	68	69	70
71	72	73	74	75	76	77	78	79	80
81	82	83	84	85	86	87	88	89	90
91	92	93	94	95	96	97	98	99	100

Hundreds Chart Puzzles

Fill in the bold squares.

								9	
								19	
	22							29	
		33			36	37	38		40
			44					49	
								59	
					66				
					75		77		
							88		
					95		97		

								8		
							17			
31					35					
	42		44							
		53								
	62									
					75					
					86					
					97					

No unauthorized copying
Games, Activities, and Puzzles

Ten-Dot Dominoes

All of these dominoes have a total of 10 dots.

☐ Draw the missing dots on the blank side.

☐ Finish the number sentence.

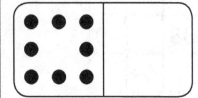 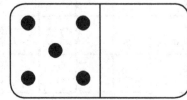 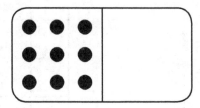

$8 +$ ☐ $= 10$ $5 +$ ☐ $= 10$ $9 +$ ☐ $= 10$

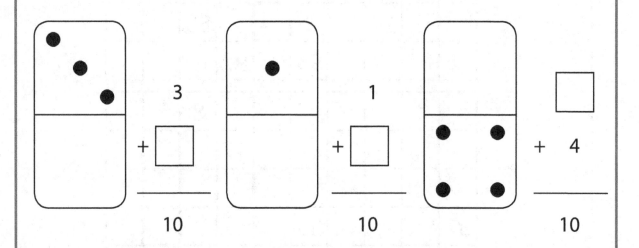

3   1   ☐

$+$ ☐ $+$ ☐ $+ \quad 4$

___   ___   ___

10   10   10

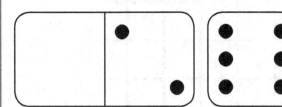 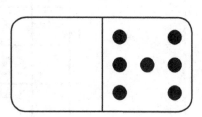

$10 =$ ☐ $+ 2$ $10 = 6 +$ ☐ $10 =$ ☐ $+ 7$

Adding Tens

$3 + 1 =$ _____

$30 + 10 =$ _____

$4 + 2 =$ _____

$40 + 20 =$ _____

$3 + 5 =$ _____

$30 + 50 =$ _____

$1 + 8 =$ _____

$10 + 80 =$ _____

$2 + 7 =$ _____

$20 + 70 =$ _____

$7 + 2 =$ _____

$70 + 20 =$ _____

$3 + 4 =$ _____

$30 + 40 =$ _____

$2 + 5 =$ _____

$20 + 50 =$ _____

$6 + 1 =$ _____

$60 + 10 =$ _____

$5 + 2 =$ _____

$50 + 20 =$ _____

Food Sale

28¢

18¢

22¢

24¢

30¢

20¢
MILK

24¢

26¢

Food Sale *(continued)*

Mona's Market

Item: _____

Price: _____

Money Given: _____

Change Received: _____

Mona's Market

Item: _____

Price: _____

Money Given: _____

Change Received: _____

Mona's Market

Item: _____

Price: _____

Money Given: _____

Change Received: _____

Mona's Market

Item: _____

Price: _____

Money Given: _____

Change Received: _____

Mona's Market

Item: _____

Price: _____

Money Given: _____

Change Received: _____

Mona's Market

Item: _____

Price: _____

Money Given: _____

Change Received: _____

Mona's Market

Item: _____

Price: _____

Money Given: _____

Change Received: _____

Mona's Market

Item: _____

Price: _____

Money Given: _____

Change Received: _____

Naming Fractions Practice

Match the circles with the fractions they show.

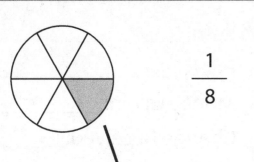

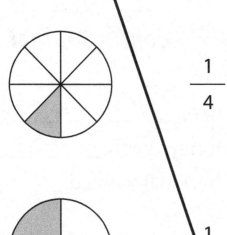

$\dfrac{1}{8}$

$\dfrac{1}{4}$

$\dfrac{1}{6}$

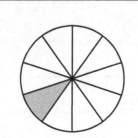

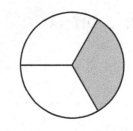

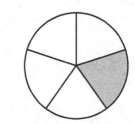

$\dfrac{1}{5}$

$\dfrac{1}{10}$

$\dfrac{1}{3}$

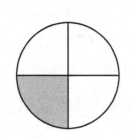

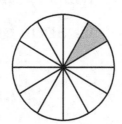

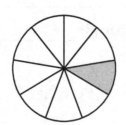

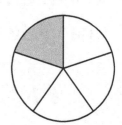

$\dfrac{1}{12}$

$\dfrac{1}{5}$

$\dfrac{1}{4}$

$\dfrac{1}{9}$

Hanji Puzzles

Circle the full rows and columns.

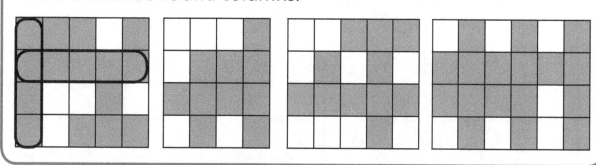

Shade the full rows and columns. Is the right number shaded in each row and column?

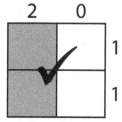

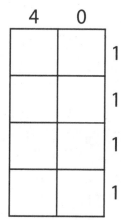

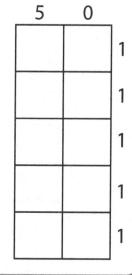

Hanji Puzzles *(continued)*

Find the rows that have enough shaded. Cross out the white squares in those rows.

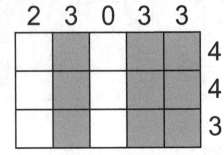

Then do the columns.

Finish solving these puzzles. Start by crossing out the squares you can't shade.

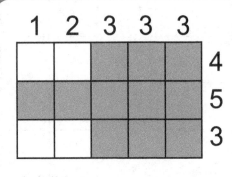

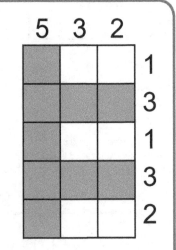

BONUS:

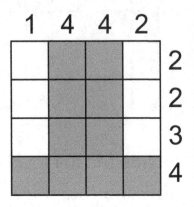

Hanji Puzzles *(continued)*

Solve the Hanji puzzles.

☐ **Step 1:** Shade the full rows and columns.

☐ **Step 2:** Cross out the squares you can't shade.

☐ **Step 3:** Finish the puzzle. Check your answer.

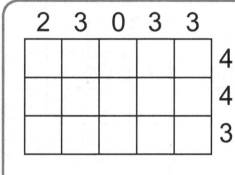

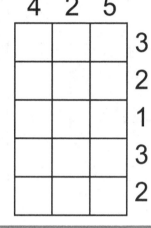

Solve the puzzle.

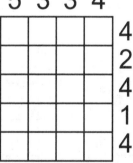

BONUS:

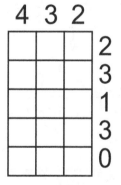

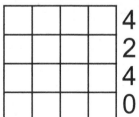

This Hanji puzzle is not possible. Can you see why?
HINT: Try solving it.

Describing Patterns in Addition Tables

Look at the shaded squares.
Describe the pattern.

+	0	1	2	3	4
0	**0**	1	2	3	4
1	1	**2**	3	4	5
2	2	3	**4**	5	6
3	3	4	5	**6**	7
4	4	5	6	7	**8**

+	0	1	2	3	4
0	0	**1**	2	3	4
1	1	2	**3**	4	5
2	2	3	4	**5**	6
3	3	4	5	6	**7**
4	4	5	6	7	8

_____ Starts at 0 _____   _____

_____ Grows by 2 _____   _____

+	0	1	2	3	4
0	0	1	2	3	**4**
1	1	2	3	**4**	5
2	2	3	**4**	5	6
3	3	**4**	5	6	7
4	**4**	5	6	7	8

+	0	1	2	3	4
0	0	1	2	3	4
1	1	2	3	4	**5**
2	2	3	4	**5**	6
3	3	4	**5**	6	7
4	4	**5**	6	7	8

_____ 4, then repeat _____   _____

_____   _____

Identifying Growing and Shrinking Patterns

Match by pattern.

1	3	5	7	9		Start at 6 Grow by 2
6	5	4	3	2	1	Start at 1 Grow by 2
6	8	10	12	14	16	Start at 16 Shrink by 4
9	6	3	0			Start at 6 Shrink by 1
16	12	8	4	0		Start at 0 Grow by 4
0	4	8	12	16		Start at 9 Shrink by 3

Patterns on Calendars

Su	M	T	W	Th	F	Sa
			1	2	3	4
5	6	7	8	9	10	11
12	13	14	15	16	17	18
19	20	21	22	23	24	25
26	27	28	29	30	31	

 Start at 26, _____

Start at 3, _____

 Start at 20, _____

Add the given numbers in the square.

6	7	8
13	14	15
20	21	22

7

13 + 14 + 15 =

+ 21

BONUS:
Find 3 more numbers in the square with the same sum.

Digital Clock Faces

A digital clock face looks like this 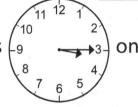 . It's a quarter past 3.

It is exactly the same as 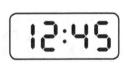 on an analogue clock.

Match the analogue clock faces to the digital times.

   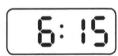

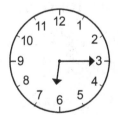   

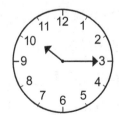   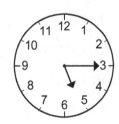

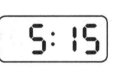

Extra Time Practice

Check the correct answer.

7:45	quarter to ✓ quarter past ____ half past ____ o'clock ____	10:15	quarter to ____ quarter past ____ half past ____ o'clock ____
3:30	quarter to ____ quarter past ____ half past ____ o'clock ____	12:00	quarter to ____ quarter past ____ half past ____ o'clock ____
8:15	quarter to ____ quarter past ____ half past ____ o'clock ____	12:45	quarter to ____ quarter past ____ half past ____ o'clock ____
6:00	quarter to ____ quarter past ____ half past ____ o'clock ____	2:30	quarter to ____ quarter past ____ half past ____ o'clock ____
5:15	quarter to ____ quarter past ____ half past ____ o'clock ____	4:45	quarter to ____ quarter past ____ half past ____ o'clock ____

How Long Is a Minute?

What can you do in a minute? Have your teacher time you.

How many times can you write your name? ☐	How many jumping jacks can you do? ☐
Count to... ☐	Write the alphabet? ☐
Sit ups? ☐	Blinks? ☐

No unauthorized copying Games, Activities, and Puzzles

UNIT 1

Number Sense 1

NS2-1 **Counting**

    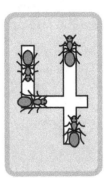 

☐ Colour.

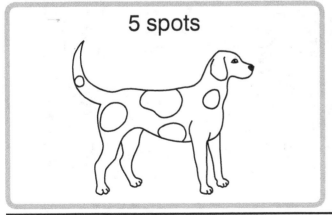

4 spots

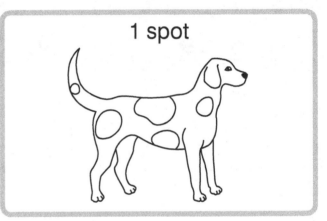

1 spot

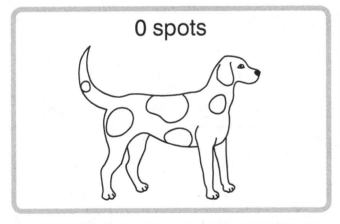

0 spots

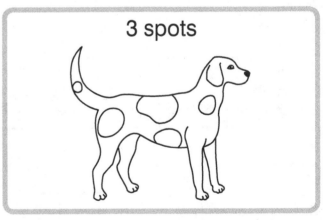

3 spots

5 spots

2 spots

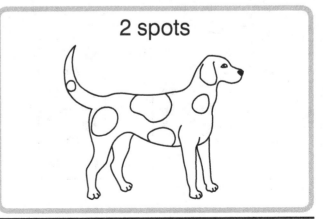

NS2-2 Matching

☐ Match by number.

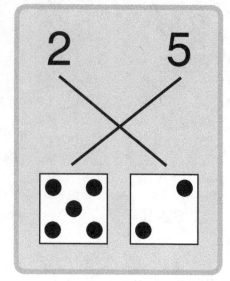

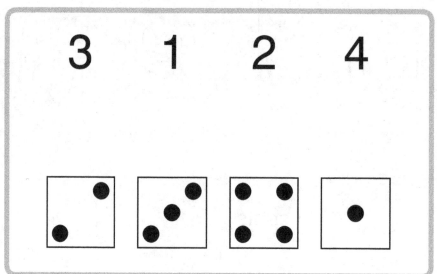

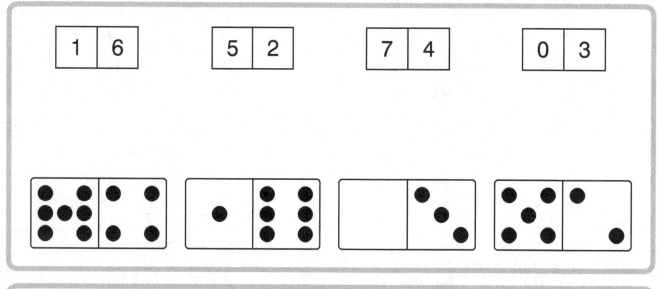

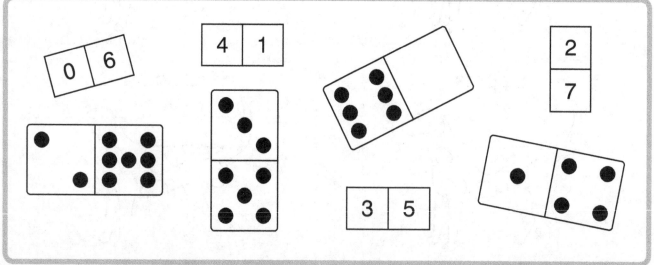

NS2-3 **One-to-One Correspondence**

☐ Circle the one that is **more**.

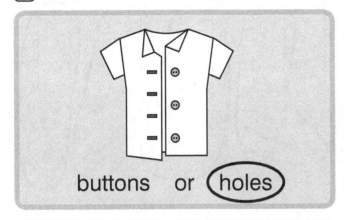

buttons   or   holes

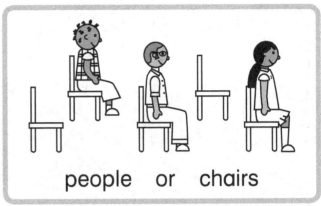

people   or   chairs

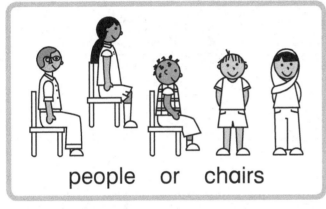

people   or   chairs

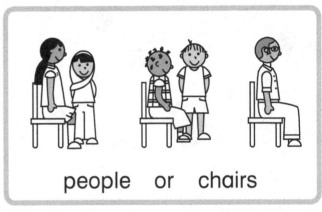

people   or   chairs

cups   or   straws

cups   or   straws

forks   or   plates

NS2-3 **One-to-One Correspondence** (continued)

☐ Pair them up to find out which is **more**.

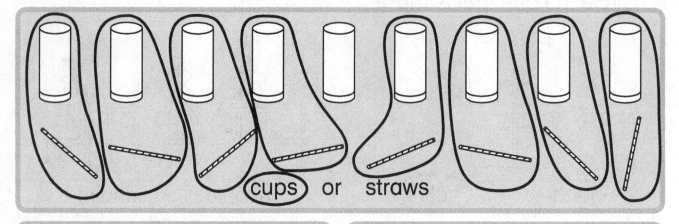

cups or straws

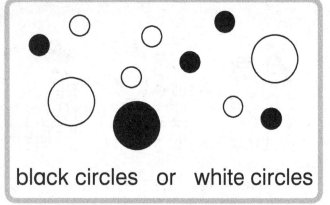

black circles or white circles

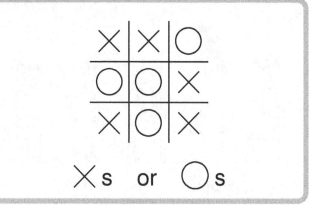

✕s or ○s

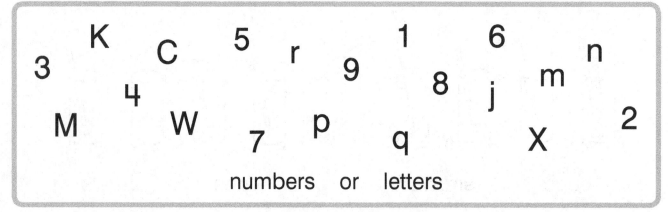

numbers or letters

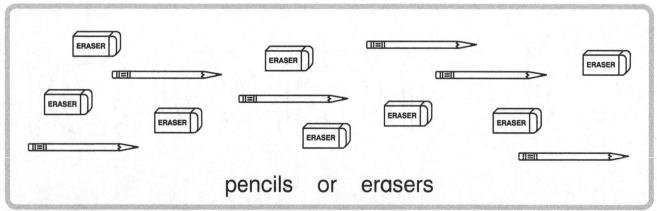

pencils or erasers

NS2-4 **Counting with a Chart**

How many ants?

1 2 3 4 5 6 7

There are __4__ ants.

1 2 3 4 5 6 7

There are ____ ants.

1 2 3 4 5 6 7

There are ____ ants.

1 2 3 4 5 6 7

There are ____ ants.

How many blocks?

| 1 | 2 | 3 | 4 | 5 | 6 | 7 | 8 | 9 | 10 |

There are ____ blocks.

| 1 | 2 | 3 | 4 | 5 | 6 | 7 | 8 | 9 | 10 |

There are ____ blocks.

| 1 | 2 | 3 | 4 | 5 | 6 | 7 | 8 | 9 | 10 |

There are ____ blocks.

No unauthorized copying

NS2-5 **How Many More?**

Write the extra numbers to find 4 more.

5 __6__ __7__ __8__ __9__

__9__ is 4 more than 5.

---

7 ___ ___ ___ ___

___ is 4 more than 7.

---

4 ___ ___ ___ ___

___ is 4 more than 4.

---

2 ___ ___ ___ ___

___ is 4 more than 2.

---

6 ___ ___ ___ ___

___ is 4 more than 6.

---

9 ___ ___ ___ ___

___ is 4 more than 9.

---

8 ___ ___ ___ ___

___ is 4 more than 8.

---

10 ___ ___ ___ ___

___ is 4 more than 10.

---

3 ___ ___ ___ ___

___ is 4 more than 3.

---

12 ___ ___ ___ ___

___ is 4 more than 12.

---

15 ___ ___ ___ ___

_____

---

11 ___ ___ ___ ___

_____

NS2-5 **How Many More?** *(continued)*

There are some apples in the bag.

How many apples altogether?

5   _6_   _7_   _8_

_8_ apples altogether.
_8_ is 3 more than 5.

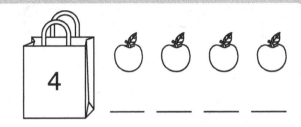

4   ___ ___ ___ ___

___ apples altogether.
___ is 4 more than 4.

3   ___ ___ ___

___ apples altogether.
___ is 3 more than 3.

2   ___ ___ ___ ___

___ apples altogether.
___ is 4 more than 2.

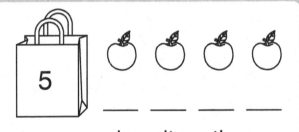

5   ___ ___ ___ ___

___ apples altogether.
___ is 4 more than 5.

8   ___

___ apples altogether.
___ is 1 more than 8.

6   ___ ___

___ apples altogether.
___ is ___ more than ___.

4   ___ ___ ___

___ apples altogether.
___ is ___ more than ___.

NS2-6 **Reading Number Words to Ten**

☐ Match the numbers to the words.

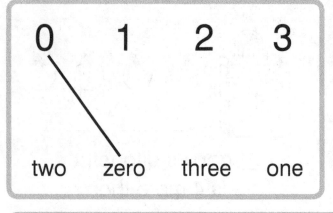

0	1	2	3
two	zero	three	one

5	6	8	9
nine	eight	six	five

4	7	6	8	3	9
seven	three	four	nine	six	eight

1	4	2	6	5	8
six	one	two	eight	four	five

7	3	9	2	1	4
three	nine	four	seven	two	one

NS2-6 **Reading Number Words to Ten** (continued)

⬜ Write the numbers above the number words.

>   8   1
>
> Rowan has eight pencils and one eraser.

Ali is nine years old and Sam is ten years old.

Pam has seven crayons, two markers, and zero pens.

Ron has five brothers and his sister has six brothers.

Lina has three sisters and her brother has four sisters.

⬜ Write your own sentence with a number word.

Have a friend write the number above the word.

NS2-7 Addition

☐ Add.

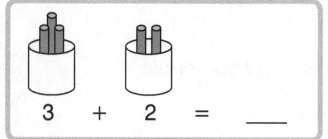

3 + 2 = ___

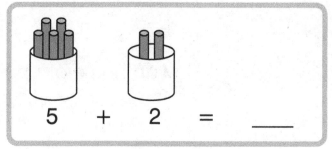

5 + 2 = ___

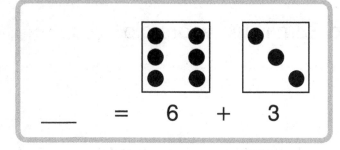

___ = 6 + 3

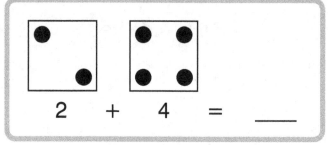

2 + 4 = ___

☐ Write the addition sentence.

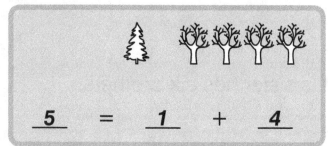

_5_ = _1_ + _4_

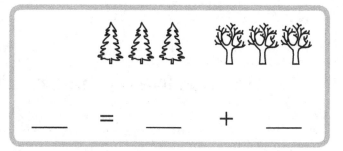

___ = ___ + ___

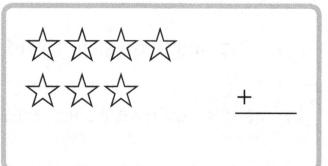

___ + ___ + ___ = ___

NS2-8 Subtraction

☐ Cross out the circles and subtract.

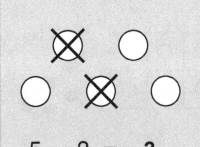

5 − 2 = __3__

4 − 3 = ___

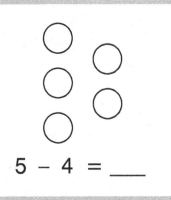

5 − 4 = ___

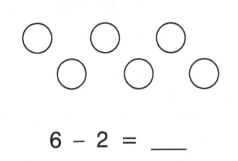

6 − 2 = ___

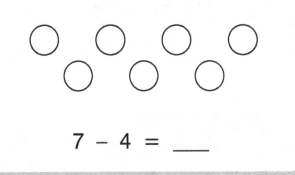

7 − 4 = ___

☐ Draw a picture to subtract.

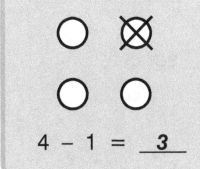

4 − 1 = __3__

5 − 3 = ___

4 − 2 = ___

6 − 3 = ___

Make your own.

NS2-9 **Counting to 20**

How many?

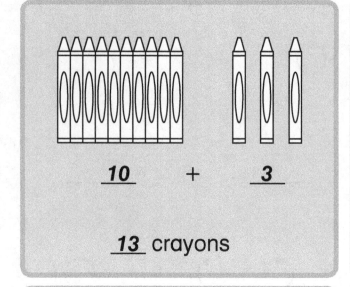
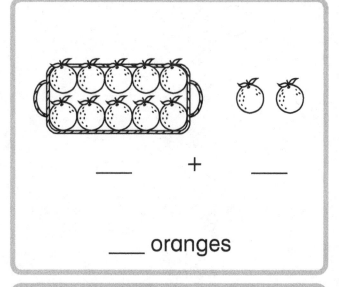
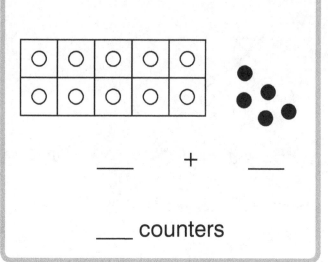
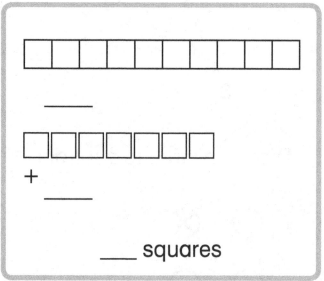
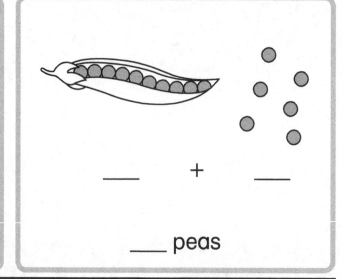

10 + **3**

13 crayons

___ + ___

___ counters

___ + ___

___ oranges

___

+

___

___ squares

___

+

___

___ apples

___ + ___

___ peas

NS2-10 Adding Using a Chart

☐ Circle the next 4 squares.
☐ Add.

| 1 | 2 | 3 | ④ | ⑤ | ⑥ | ⑦ | 8 | 9 | 10 |

$3 + 4 = \underline{\ 7\ }$

| 1 | 2 | 3 | 4 | 5 | 6 | 7 | 8 | 9 | 10 |

$2 + 4 = \underline{\quad}$

| 1 | 2 | 3 | 4 | 5 | 6 | 7 | 8 | 9 | 10 |

$6 + 4 = \underline{\quad}$

| 1 | 2 | 3 | 4 | 5 | 6 | 7 | 8 | 9 | 10 |
| 11 | 12 | 13 | 14 | 15 | 16 | 17 | 18 | 19 | 20 |

$9 + 4 = \underline{\quad}$

| 1 | 2 | 3 | 4 | 5 | 6 | 7 | 8 | 9 | 10 |
| 11 | 12 | 13 | 14 | 15 | 16 | 17 | 18 | 19 | 20 |

$8 + 4 = \underline{\quad}$

NS2-10 Adding Using a Chart (continued)

Use the reading pattern.

☐ Shade the first number of squares.
☐ Circle the second number of squares.
☐ Add.

1	2	3	4	5	6	7	8	9	10
11	12	13	14	15	16	17	18	19	20

7 + 6 = **13**

1	2	3	4	5	6	7	8	9	10
11	12	13	14	15	16	17	18	19	20

6 + 9 = ____

1	2	3	4	5	6	7	8	9	10
11	12	13	14	15	16	17	18	19	20

8 + 8 = ____

1	2	3	4	5	6	7	8	9	10
11	12	13	14	15	16	17	18	19	20

7 + 9 = ____

1	2	3	4	5	6	7	8	9	10
11	12	13	14	15	16	17	18	19	20

9 + 4 = ____

NS2-10 Adding Using a Chart *(continued)*

Isobel **pretends** the first number of squares are shaded.
Then she circles the second number of squares.

| 1 | 2 | 3 | 4 | ⑤ | ⑥ | ⑦ | 8 | 9 | 10 |

$4 + 3 = \underline{7}$

☐ Use Isobel's method to add.

| 1 | 2 | 3 | 4 | 5 | ⑥ | ⑦ | 8 | 9 | 10 |

$5 + 2 = \underline{}$

| 1 | 2 | 3 | ④ | ⑤ | ⑥ | ⑦ | ⑧ | ⑨ | 10 |

$3 + 6 = \underline{}$

| 1 | 2 | 3 | 4 | 5 | 6 | 7 | 8 | 9 | 10 |

$4 + 2 = \underline{}$

| 1 | 2 | 3 | 4 | 5 | 6 | 7 | 8 | 9 | 10 |

$5 + 3 = \underline{}$

| 1 | 2 | 3 | 4 | 5 | 6 | 7 | 8 | 9 | 10 |
| 11 | 12 | 13 | 14 | 15 | 16 | 17 | 18 | 19 | 20 |

$7 + 5 = \underline{}$

Number Sense 1

NS2-10 **Adding Using a Chart** *(continued)*

☐ Add.

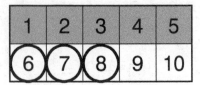

5 + 3 = _____

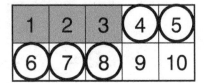

3 + 5 = _____

1	2	3	4	5
6	7	8	9	10

6 + 2 = _____

1	2	3	4	5
6	7	8	9	10

2 + 6 = _____

1	2	3	4	5	6	7	8	9	10
11	12	13	14	15	16	17	18	19	20

5 + 9 = _____

1	2	3	4	5	6	7	8	9	10
11	12	13	14	15	16	17	18	19	20

9 + 5 = _____

What do you notice? _____

_____

NS2-11 Tens and Ones Blocks

One row of 10 and how many more ones?

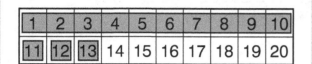

13 =

1 row of 10 + ___ more ones

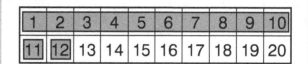

12 =

1 row of 10 + ___ more ones

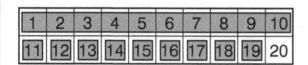

19 =

1 row of 10 + ___ more ones

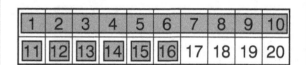

16 =

1 row of 10 + ___ more ones

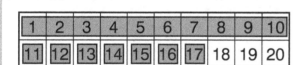

17 =

1 row of 10 + ___ more ones

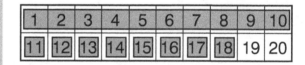

18 =

1 row of 10 + ___ more ones

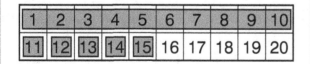

15 =

1 row of 10 + ___ more ones

14 =

1 row of 10 + ___ more ones

NS2-11 **Tens and Ones Blocks** *(continued)*

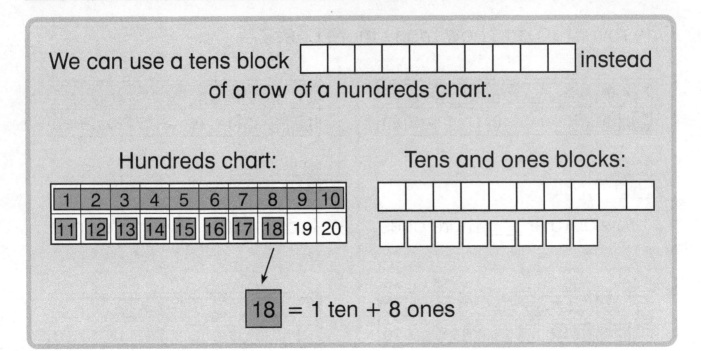

We can use a tens block [   ] instead of a row of a hundreds chart.

Hundreds chart:

1	2	3	4	5	6	7	8	9	10
11	12	13	14	15	16	17	18	19	20

Tens and ones blocks:

18 = 1 ten + 8 ones

What number do the blocks show?

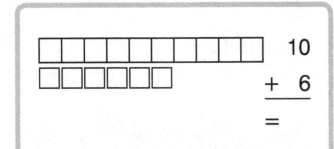

10
+ 6
=

10
+ 1
=

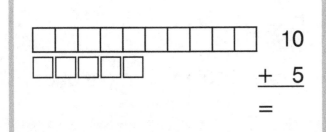

10
+ 5
=

10
+ 3
=

10
+ 9
=

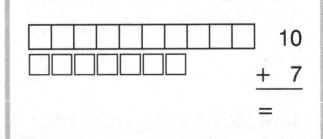

10
+ 7
=

NS2-12 Reading Number Words to Twenty

☐ Underline the beginning letters that are the same.

six **_six_**teen	two twelve
three thirteen	four fourteen
eight eighteen	five fifteen

☐ Circle the digits that are the same.

② 1②	6 16	7 17
9 19	8 18	3 13

☐ Underline and circle the same parts.

_th_ree = ③ **_th_**irteen = 1③	four = 4 fourteen = 14
five = 5 fifteen = 15	nine = 9 nineteen = 19
seven = 7 seventeen = 17	two = 2 twelve = 12

NS2-12 **Reading Number Words to Twenty** *(continued)*

☐ Write the numbers.

thirteen = _1_ _3_	**seven**teen = __ __	**fi**fteen = __ __
sixteen = __ __	fourteen = __ __	twelve = __ __
nineteen = __ __	eighteen = __ __	eleven = __ __

☐ Match the word with the number.

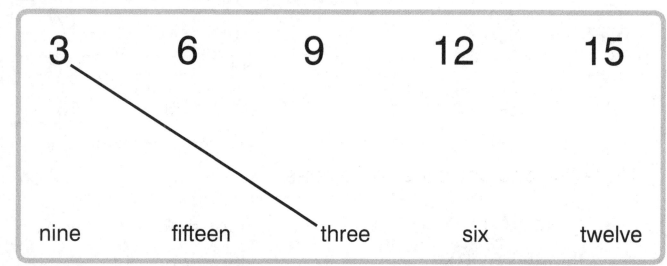

3	6	9	12	15
nine	fifteen	three	six	twelve

11	13	15	17	19
fifteen	nineteen	thirteen	eleven	seventeen

NS2-12 **Reading Number Words to Twenty** (continued)

☐ Write the number above the number word.

13 Dora is thirteen months old.	Miki has twenty teeth.
Sixteen friends played tag.	Holidays start in eleven days.

We played basketball for fifteen minutes.

Curtis invited eighteen friends to his birthday party.

Bonus

Pam's soccer team has twelve players — seven girls and five boys.

☐ Write your own sentence with a number word.

Have a partner write the number above the word.

NS2-13 **First Word Problems**

☐ Add using the pictures.

1 car   2 more cars

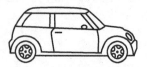    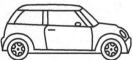

$$1 + 2 = \underline{\hspace{1cm}}$$

2 cars   3 more cars

$$2 + 3 = \underline{\hspace{1cm}}$$

5 cars   3 more cars

$$5 + 3 = \underline{\hspace{1cm}}$$

2 cars   6 more cars

$$2 + 6 = \underline{\hspace{1cm}}$$

NS2-13 **First Word Problems** *(continued)*

☐ Write the numbers above the number words.
☐ Draw counters to show the numbers.
☐ Write the number sentence.
☐ Write the answer as a word.

3
There are three cats.   ○ ○ ○

4
There are four dogs.   ○ ○ ○ ○

There are _____**seven**_____ animals altogether.

3
+ 4
7

There are six yellow crayons.

There are five blue crayons.

There are _____ crayons in total.

+

There are two big toys.

There are eight small toys.

There are _____ toys in total.

+

Zia has seven shirts.

John has six shirts.

They have _____ shirts altogether.

+

NS2-13 First Word Problems *(continued)*

☐ Write the numbers above the number words.
☐ Draw circles and cross some out to subtract.
☐ Write the subtraction sentence.
☐ Write the answer as a word.

8
Jason had eight crayons.   ⊗⊗⊗○○○○○ | 8 |

3
He gave three to his sister.   − | 3 |

Jason has ____*five*____ crayons left. | 5 |

Guled had four pencils.

He lost one of them.

Guled has _____ pencils left.

Lina had six marbles.

She gave two to Rosa.

Lina has _____ marbles left.

Ron had five toy cars.

His teacher took three of them.

Now Ron has _____ toy cars.

NS2-13 First Word Problems *(continued)*

◯ Circle what is different in the two sentences.
◯ Draw a model.
◯ Write a sentence to describe how many more.

(Sarah) has (5) marbles.
(Ron) has (9) marbles.

_____ **Ron has 4 more marbles than Sarah** _____.

Sarah has 8 apples.
Ron has 3 apples.

_____ **has** _____ **more apples than** _____.

Jason has 5 pencils.
Dmitri has 7 pencils.

_____ **has** _____ **more** _____ **than** _____.

Rita ate 6 berries.
Pam ate 8 berries.

_____ **ate** _____.

Mary spent 9 dimes.
Lina spent 6 dimes.

_____.

NS2-13 First Word Problems *(continued)*

☐ Circle what is different in the two sentences.
☐ Draw a model.
☐ Write a sentence to describe how many more.

Sarah has ⑦ apples.
Sarah has ⑨ pears.

Sarah has 2 more pears than apples.

Sarah has 5 apples.
Sarah has 8 pears.

Sarah has ___ more ___ pears ___ apples .

Miki has 7 markers.
Miki has 4 crayons.

Miki has ___ more ___ than ___ .

Bilal has 9 nickels.
Bilal has 2 pennies.

_____.

Katie has 8 toy trucks.
Katie has 3 toy cars.

_____.

NS2-14 Making Word Problems

☐ Add.
☐ Write what you are adding.

There are 5 big frogs.

There are 2 small frogs.

There are __7__ _____*frogs*_____ altogether.

There are 4 new pencils.

There are 2 used pencils.

There are ___ _____ altogether.

There are 5 green apples.

There are 5 red apples.

There are ___ _____ altogether.

There are 3 empty cups.

There are 2 full cups.

There are ___ _____ altogether.

✓NS2-14 Making Word Problems *(continued)*

☐ Use the words to make a problem for each picture.

~~big~~	~~small~~	empty	full
farm	zoo	happy	sad

There are __3__ _____big_____ frogs.

There are __2__ ____small____ frogs.

There are __5__ frogs altogether.

There are __3__ ___oltah___ bowls.

There are __2__ ___frehly___ bowls.

There are __5__ bowls altogether.

There are __2__ ___spotd___ animals.

There are __3__ ___furld___ animals.

There are __5__ animals altogether.

There are __4__ ___happ___ faces.

There are __3__ ___sad___ faces.

There are __7__ faces altogether.

NS2-14 Making Word Problems *(continued)*

☐ Write a problem for each picture.
☐ Write the subtraction sentence.

There were 10 flies.

The frog ate 3 of them.

How many are left?

$\underline{10} - \underline{3} = \underline{7}$

Ther were 9 plies.
Thy froy ate 4 ofthtnem
h0ow many are left?

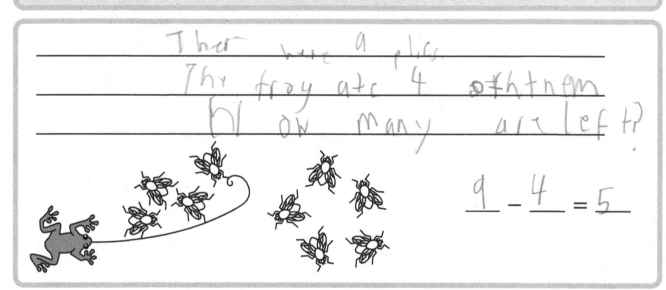

$\underline{9} - \underline{4} = 5$

Thell are 1 flies.
one frog ate 2
How many are left?

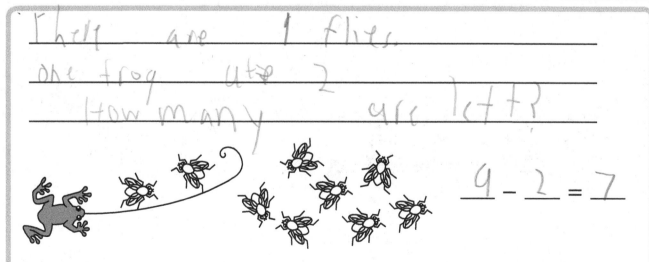

$\underline{9} - \underline{2} = 7$

NS2-14 Making Word Problems (continued)

☐ Write a problem for each picture.
☐ Write the subtraction sentence.

There were 9 apples in the tree.

4 of them fell.

How many are left?

$\underline{9} - \underline{4} = \underline{5}$

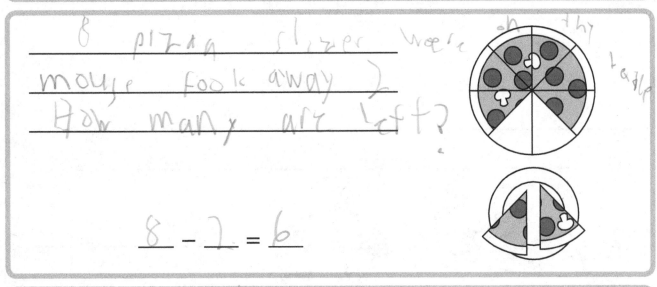

8 pizza slizes were
mouse took away)
How many are left?

$\underline{8} - \underline{2} = \underline{6}$

7 birds sat on a tree
3 run away
How many are left?

$\underline{7} - \underline{4} = \underline{4}$

NS2-15 **Counting to 100**

How many crayons?

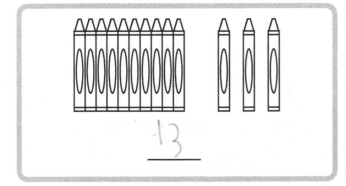

13

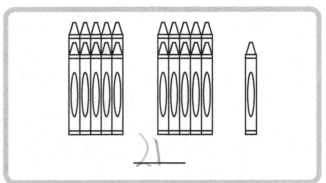

21

34

53

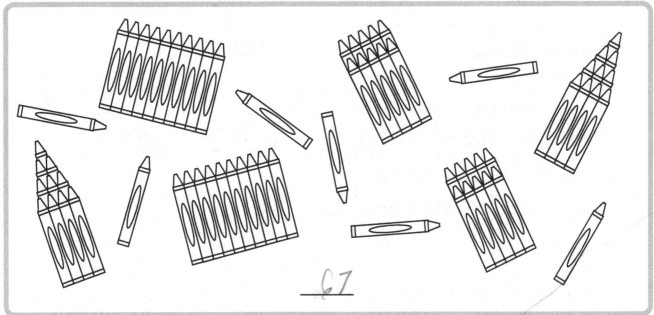

67

NS2-16 **More Tens and Ones Blocks**

☐ Fill in the chart.
☐ Write the number shown.

tens	ones
3	4

Number: __34__

tens	ones

Number: _____

tens	ones

Number: _____

tens	ones

Number: _____

☐ Show each number using blocks. 50 43 37 19 32

NS2-17 Ordering Numbers to 100

☐ Circle the numbers on the number line.
☐ Write the numbers from smallest to largest.

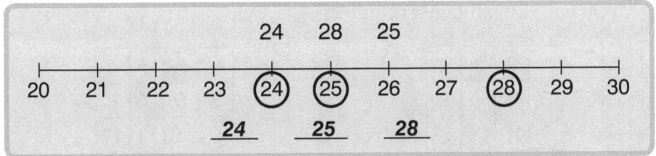

24   28   25

20 21 22 23 ⟨24⟩ ⟨25⟩ 26 27 ⟨28⟩ 29 30

__24__   __25__   __28__

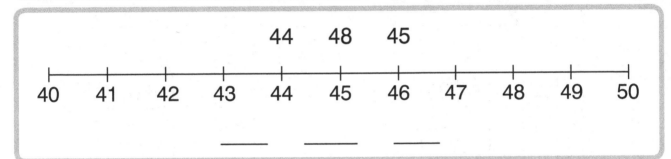

44   48   45

40 41 42 43 44 45 46 47 48 49 50

____   ____   ____

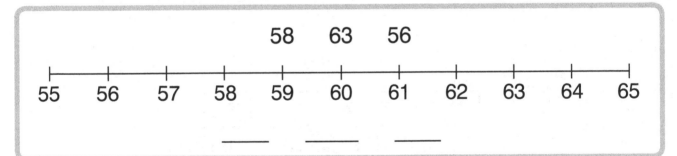

58   63   56

55 56 57 58 59 60 61 62 63 64 65

____   ____   ____

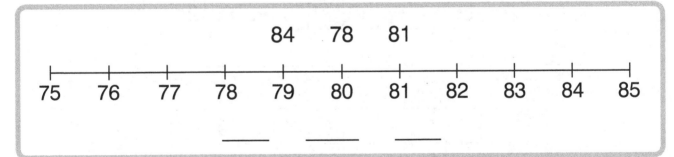

84   78   81

75 76 77 78 79 80 81 82 83 84 85

____   ____   ____

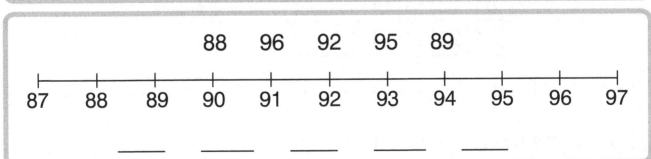

88   96   92   95   89

87 88 89 90 91 92 93 94 95 96 97

____ ____ ____ ____ ____

NS2-17 Ordering Numbers to 100 (continued)

☐ Write the shaded numbers in order.
Use the reading pattern.
Start with the smallest number.

1	2	**3**	4
5	6	7	8
9	10	**11**	12

__3__ __9__ __11__

1	**2**	3	4
5	6	**7**	8
9	10	11	12

___ ___ ___

31	32	33	**34**	35
36	37	38	39	40
41	42	**43**	44	45

___ ___ ___

53	54	**55**	56	57
58	59	60	61	**62**
63	**64**	65	66	67

___ ___ ___

65	**66**	67	68	69	70	71	**72**	73	74
75	76	**77**	78	79	**80**	81	82	83	**84**
85	86	87	88	89	**90**	91	92	93	94

___ ___ ___ ___ ___ ___

1	2	**3**	4	5	6	7	8	9	**10**
11	12	13	14	15	**16**	17	18	19	20
21	22	23	24	**25**	26	27	28	**29**	30

___ ___ ___ ___ ___ ___

☐ Use a metre stick to check your answers.

NS2-18 Using Length to Add and Subtract

☐ Add.

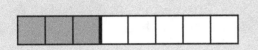

$3 + 5 = \underline{\ 8\ }$

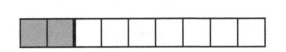

$2 + 7 = \underline{\ \ \ }$

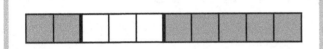

$2 + 3 + 5 = \underline{\ \ \ }$

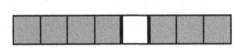

$4 + 1 + 3 = \underline{\ \ \ }$

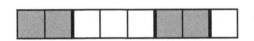

$2 + 3 + 2 + 1 = \underline{\ \ \ }$

$1 + 4 + 3 + 2 = \underline{\ \ \ }$

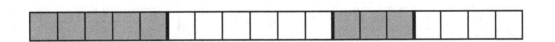

$5 + 6 + 3 + 4 = \underline{\ \ \ }$

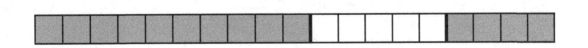

$10 + 5 + 4 = \underline{\ \ \ }$

No unauthorized copying   **Number Sense 1**

NS2-18 **Using Length to Add and Subtract** *(continued)*

☐ Use the model to subtract.

$6 - 2 =$ __4__

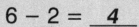

$7 - 4 =$ _____

$7 - 1 =$ _____

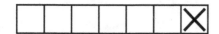

$6 - 3 =$ _____

☐ Finish the model to subtract.

$7 - 3 =$ _____

$7 - 2 =$ _____

$10 - 4 =$ _____

NS2-19 Missing Numbers

☐ Write the missing number.

2 + 3 + ____

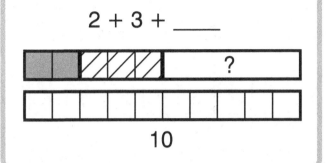

10

2 + 2 + ____

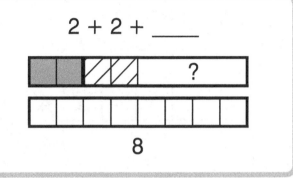

8

1 + ____ + 4

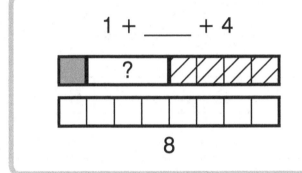

8

4 + ____ + 4

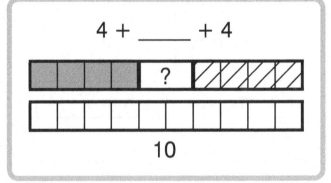

10

1 + ____ + 6

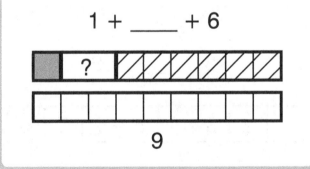

9

____ + 3 + 3

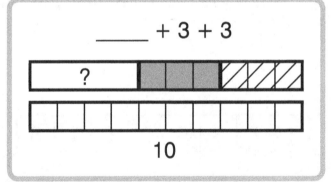

10

2 + 4 + ____

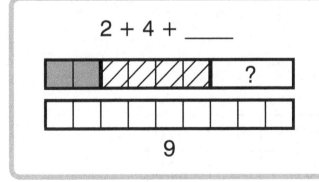

9

3 + ____ + 1

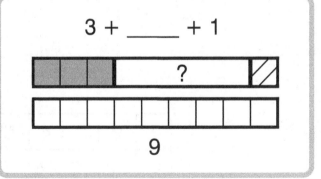

9

📓 Make up your own problem and solve it using number blocks.

NS2-19 **Missing Numbers** (continued)

☐ Find the missing number.

6 – __2__ = 4

1	2	3	4	5̶	6̶

7 – ___ = 4

1	2	3	4	5̶	6̶	7̶

7 – ___ = 5

1	2	3	4	5	6̶	7̶

6 – ___ = 3

1	2	3	4̶	5̶	6̶

☐ Finish the model to find the missing number.

8 – ___ = 3

1	2	3	4	5	6	7	8

8 – ___ = 6

1	2	3	4	5	6	7	8

20 – ___ = 7

1	2	3	4	5	6	7	8	9	10
11	12	13	14	15	16	17	18	19	20

NS2-19 **Missing Numbers** (continued)

⬜ Find the missing number.

$$2 + 5 = 10 - \underline{\ 3\ }$$

2 + 5

10 − ⬜

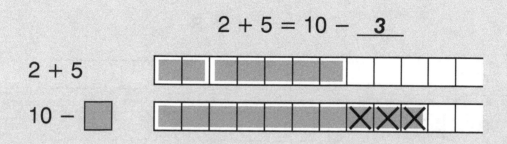

$$7 - 3 = 10 - \underline{\ \ \ \ }$$

7 − 3

10 − ⬜

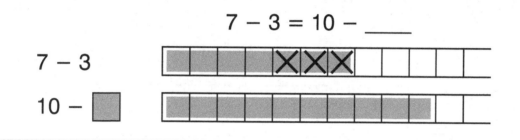

$$9 - \underline{\ \ \ \ } = 4 + 2$$

4 + 2

9 − ⬜

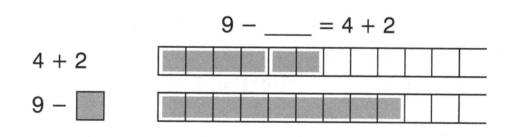

$$10 - 4 = 2 + \underline{\ \ \ \ }$$

10 − 4

2 + ⬜

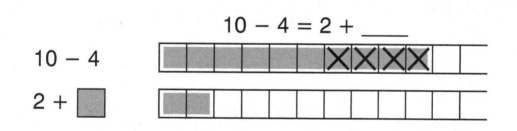

$$11 - 6 = 9 - \underline{\ \ \ \ }$$

11 − 6

9 − ⬜

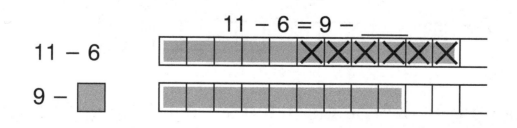

NS2-19 **Missing Numbers** (continued)

☐ Draw a model to find the missing number.

$$4 + 1 = 8 - \underline{\quad}$$

4 + 1

8 − ▪

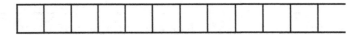
$$7 - 2 = 1 + \underline{\quad}$$

7 − 2

1 + ▪

$$5 + 6 = 7 + \underline{\quad}$$

5 + 6

7 + ▪

$$10 - 5 = 7 - \underline{\quad}$$

10 − 5

7 − ▪

📓 Make up your own problem and solve it using grid paper.

NS2-20 Adding, Subtracting, and Order

The dominoes got turned around.

⬜ Write one addition sentence for both pictures.

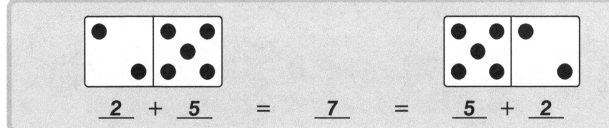

_2_ + _5_ = _7_ = _5_ + _2_

___ + ___ = ___ = ___ + ___

___ + ___ = ___ = ___ + ___

___ + ___ = ___ = ___ + ___

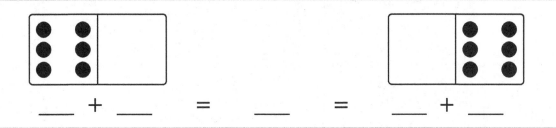

___ + ___ = ___ = ___ + ___

📓 Rita says 34 + 17 = 17 + 34. Explain why she is right.

NS2-20 **Adding, Subtracting, and Order** (continued)

How many buttons altogether?

☐ Find the total in 6 different ways.

total							

10	=	**2**	+	**5**	+	**3**	

total							

___	=	___	+	___	+	___	

total							

___	=	___	+	___	+	___	

total							

___	=	___	+	___	+	___	

total							

___	=	___	+	___	+	___	

total							
___	=	___	+	___	+	___	

NS2-21 Adding with a Number Line

The frog takes 2 leaps. Where does it end up?

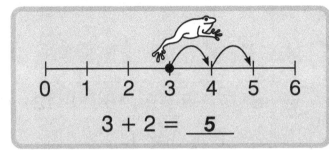

$$3 + 2 = \underline{\ 5\ }$$

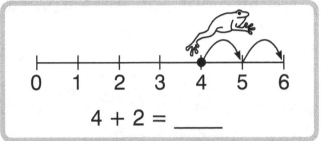

$$4 + 2 = \underline{\qquad}$$

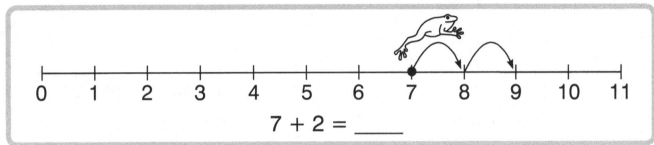

$$7 + 2 = \underline{\qquad}$$

☐ Trace 3 leaps.
☐ Add 3.

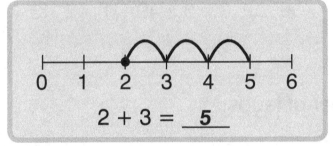

$$2 + 3 = \underline{\ 5\ }$$

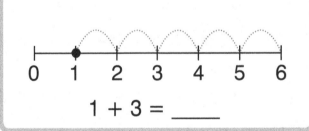

$$1 + 3 = \underline{\qquad}$$

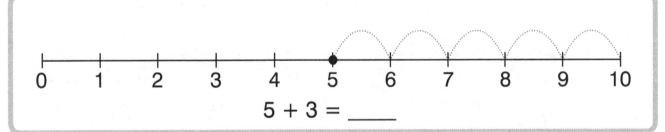

$$5 + 3 = \underline{\qquad}$$

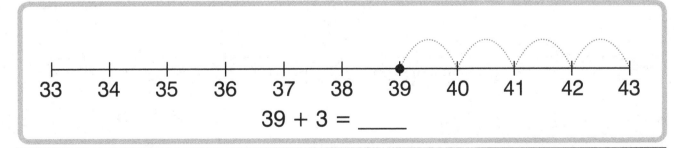

$$39 + 3 = \underline{\qquad}$$

NS2-21 **Adding with a Number Line** (continued)

The frog starts at the first number.

☐ Draw a dot where the frog starts.

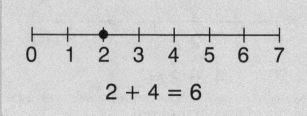

$2 + 4 = 6$

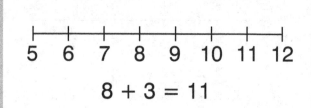

$8 + 3 = 11$

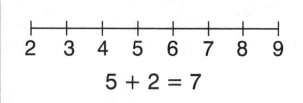

$5 + 2 = 7$

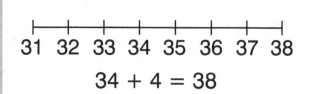

$34 + 4 = 38$

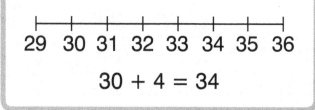

$30 + 4 = 34$

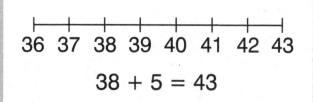

$38 + 5 = 43$

The frog jumps the second number of leaps.

☐ Draw the frog's leaps.

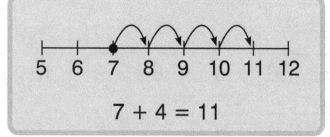

$7 + 4 = 11$

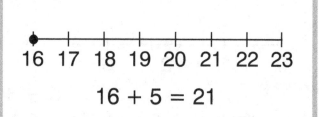

$16 + 5 = 21$

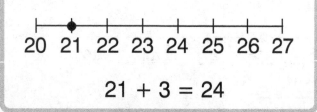

$21 + 3 = 24$

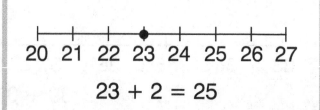

$23 + 2 = 25$

NS2-21 **Adding with a Number Line** (continued)

☐ Use a number line to add.

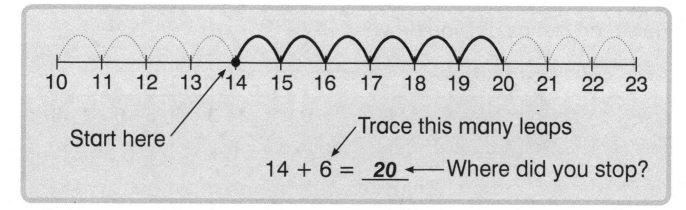

Start here

Trace this many leaps

$14 + 6 = $ **_20_** ← Where did you stop?

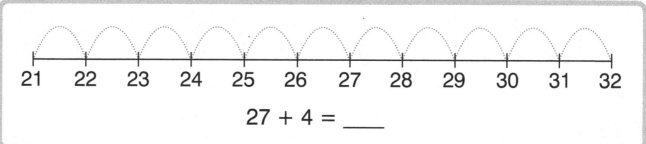

$27 + 4 = $ ____

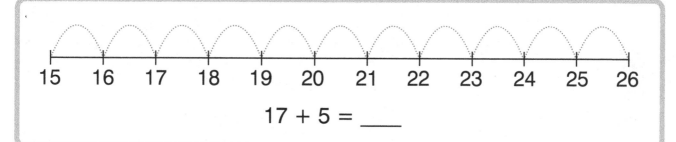

$17 + 5 = $ ____

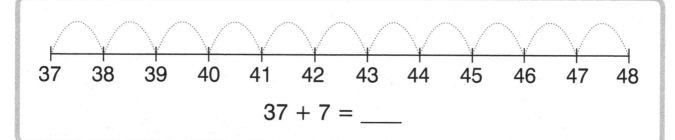

$37 + 7 = $ ____

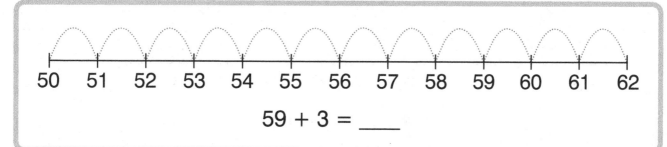

$59 + 3 = $ ____

NS2-21 **Adding with a Number Line** *(continued)*

☐ Draw the leaps from the first dot to the second dot.

How many leaps did you draw?

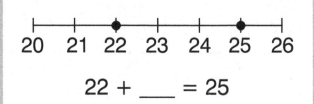

$3 + \underline{\ 4\ } = 7$

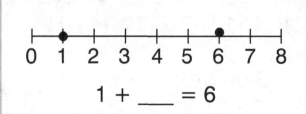

$1 + \underline{\ \ \ } = 6$

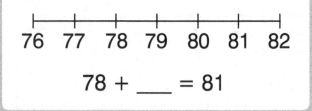

$2 + \underline{\ \ \ } = 8$

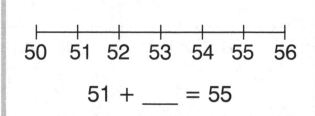

$22 + \underline{\ \ \ } = 25$

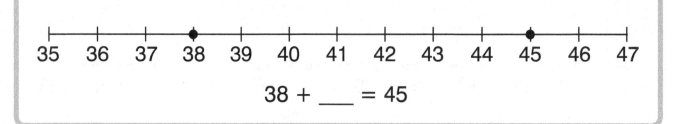

$38 + \underline{\ \ \ } = 45$

☐ Find the missing number by using a number line.

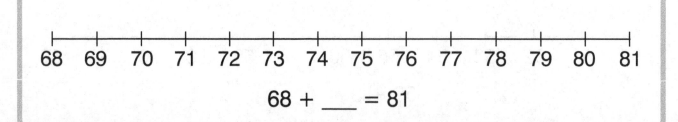

$78 + \underline{\ \ \ } = 81$

$51 + \underline{\ \ \ } = 55$

$68 + \underline{\ \ \ } = 81$

NS2-22 Adding by Counting On

☐ Colour the next circle.
☐ Add 1.

1	2	3	4	5	6	7	8	9	10	11	12
●	●	●	●	●	●	●	●	◉	○	○	○

$$8 + 1 = \underline{\ 9\ }$$

1	2	3	4	5	6	7	8	9	10	11	12
●	●	●	●	●	●	●	●	●	●	○	○

$$10 + 1 = \underline{\qquad}$$

1	2	3	4	5	6	7	8	9	10	11	12
●	●	●	●	●	○	○	○	○	○	○	○

$$5 + 1 = \underline{\qquad}$$

☐ Find the next number.
☐ Add 1.

1　2　3　**4**　5　6　7

$$4 + 1 = \underline{\qquad}$$

1　2　3　4　5　**6**　7

$$6 + 1 = \underline{\qquad}$$

$$9 + 1 = \underline{\qquad}$$

$$11 + 1 = \underline{\qquad}$$

$$17 + 1 = \underline{\qquad}$$

NS2-22 **Adding by Counting On** (continued)

☐ Find the next 2 numbers.
☐ Add 2.

1   2   3   **4**   5   6   7   8

$$4 + 2 = \underline{\;6\;}$$

1   2   3   4   5   **6**   7   8

$$6 + 2 = \underline{\;\;\;}$$

1   2   **3**   4   5   6   7   8

$$3 + 2 = \underline{\;\;\;}$$

1   2   3   4   **5**   6   7   8

$$5 + 2 = \underline{\;\;\;}$$

☐ Write the next 2 numbers to add 2.

7 ___ ___ so 7 + 2 = ___

10 ___ ___ so 10 + 2 = ___

15 ___ ___ so 15 + 2 = ___

89 ___ ___ so 89 + 2 = ___

☐ Write the next 5 numbers to add 5.

2 ___ ___ ___ ___ ___ so 2 + 5 = ___

6 ___ ___ ___ ___ ___ so 6 + 5 = ___

18 ___ ___ ___ ___ ___ so 18 + 5 = ___

NS2-22 Adding by Counting On *(continued)*

☐ Start at the first number.
☐ Trace the second number of blanks.
☐ Add by counting on.

| 5 | _6_ | _7_ | _8_ | _9_ | _10_ | _11_ | ___ | 5 + 6 = _11_ |

| ☐ | __ __ __ __ __ __ __ __ | 8 + 2 = ___ |

| ☐ | __ __ __ __ __ __ __ __ | 21 + 4 = ___ |

☐ Use your fingers to add by counting on.

| 37 | _38_ | _39_ | _40_ | _41_ | so | 37 + 4 = 41 |

| 45 + 3 = ___ | 58 + 4 = ___ | 69 + 2 = ___ |

| 38 + 3 = ___ | 29 + 2 = ___ | 35 + 4 = ___ |

| 84 + 9 = ___ | 75 + 7 = ___ | 57 + 7 = ___ |

NS2-22 **Adding by Counting On** (continued)

☐ Draw the correct number of blanks.
☐ Add by counting on in two ways.

7 + 3 = __10__

7   _8_   _9_   _10_   __   __   __   __   __   __

3   _4_   _5_   _6_   _7_   _8_   _9_   _10_   __   __   __

2 + 5 = ___

2   __ __ __ __ __ __ __ __ __

5   __ __ __ __ __ __ __ __ __

9 + 3 = ___

9   __ __ __ __ __ __ __ __ __

3   __ __ __ __ __ __ __ __ __

4 + 8 = ___

4   __ __ __ __ __ __ __ __ __

8   __ __ __ __ __ __ __ __ __

☐ What is easier, counting on from the **bigger** number or from the **smaller** number? Explain.

_____

_____

_____

NS2-22 **Adding by Counting On** (continued)

◯ Count from the first number to the second number.
◯ Find the missing number.

| 5 | _6_ _7_ _8_ _9_ _10_ _11_ ___ ___ ___ ___ |

$$5 + \underline{6} = 11$$

| 17 | ___ ___ ___ ___ ___ ___ ___ ___ ___ ___ |

$$17 + \underline{} = 22$$

| ☐ | ___ ___ ___ ___ ___ ___ ___ ___ ___ ___ |

$$32 + \underline{} = 36$$

| ☐ | ___ ___ ___ ___ ___ ___ ___ ___ ___ ___ |

$$19 + \underline{} = 28$$

| ☐ | ___ ___ ___ ___ ___ ___ ___ ___ ___ ___ |

$$25 + \underline{} = 32$$

| ☐ | ___ ___ ___ ___ ___ ___ ___ ___ ___ ___ |

$$76 + \underline{} = 84$$

📓 Make up your own problem and solve it.

NS2-23 Subtracting with a Number Line

The frog takes 2 leaps back. Where does it end up?

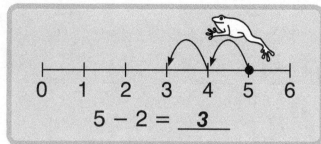

$5 - 2 = \underline{\quad 3 \quad}$

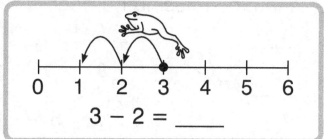

$3 - 2 = \underline{\qquad}$

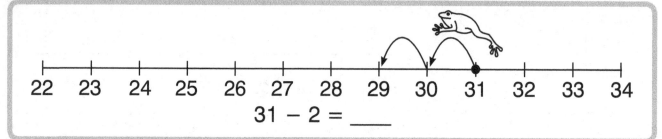

$31 - 2 = \underline{\qquad}$

☐ Trace 3 leaps back.
☐ Subtract 3.

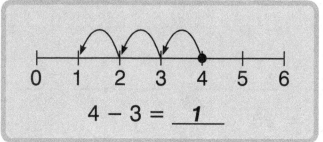

$4 - 3 = \underline{\quad 1 \quad}$

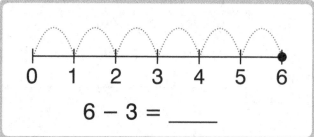

$6 - 3 = \underline{\qquad}$

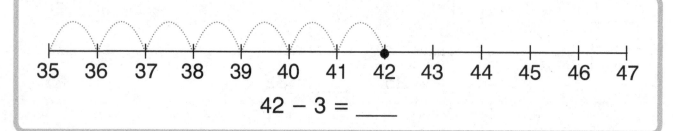

$42 - 3 = \underline{\qquad}$

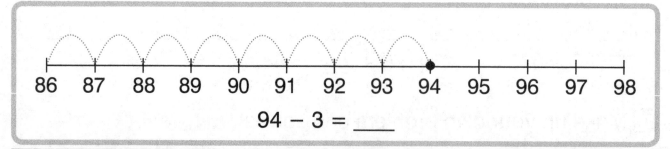

$94 - 3 = \underline{\qquad}$

NS2-23 **Subtracting with a Number Line** (continued)

The frog starts at the first number.

⬜ Draw a dot where the frog starts.

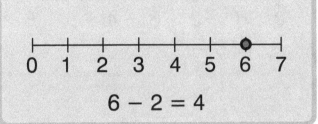

$6 - 2 = 4$

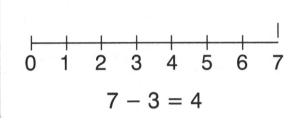

$7 - 3 = 4$

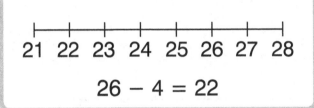

$26 - 4 = 22$

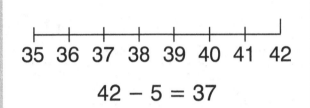

$42 - 5 = 37$

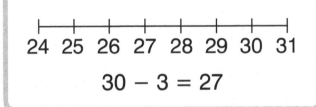

$30 - 3 = 27$

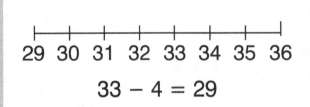

$33 - 4 = 29$

The frog jumps back the second number of leaps.

⬜ Draw the frog's leaps.

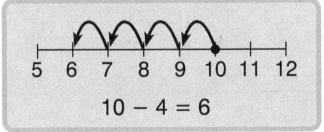

$10 - 4 = 6$

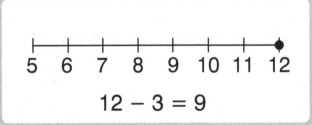

$12 - 3 = 9$

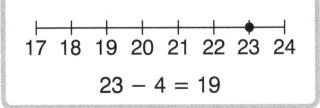

$23 - 4 = 19$

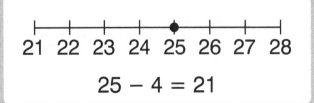

$25 - 4 = 21$

NS2-23 **Subtracting with a Number Line** (continued)

☐ Use a number line to subtract.

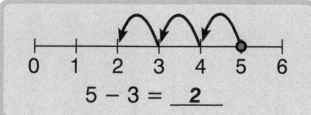

$5 - 3 =$ __2__

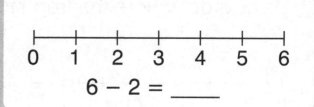

$6 - 2 =$ ____

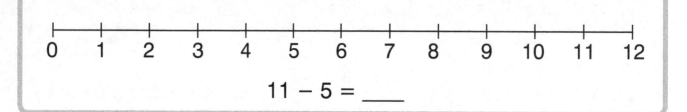

$11 - 5 =$ ____

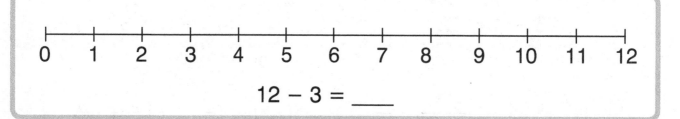

$12 - 3 =$ ____

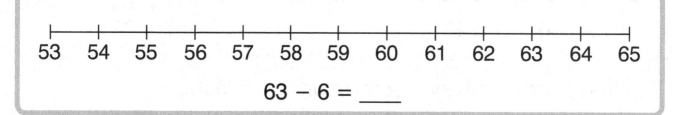

$63 - 6 =$ ____

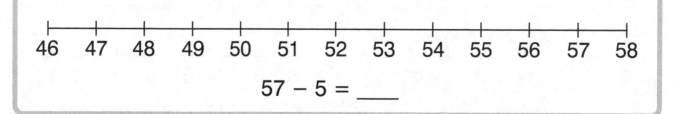

$57 - 5 =$ ____

Make your own.

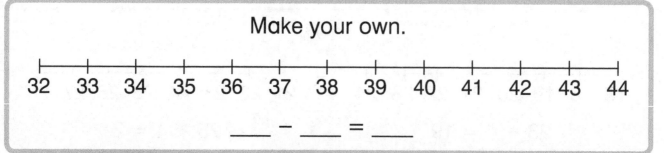

____ − ____ = ____

NS2-23 **Subtracting with a Number Line** (continued)

☐ Draw the leaps from the second dot to the first dot.
☐ How many leaps did you draw? Fill in the blank.

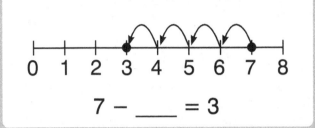

$$7 - \_\_\_ = 3$$

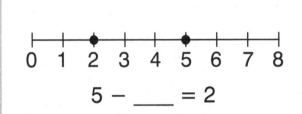

$$5 - \_\_\_ = 2$$

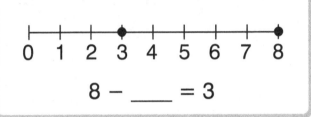

$$8 - \_\_\_ = 3$$

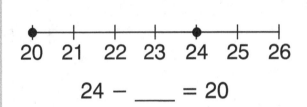

$$24 - \_\_\_ = 20$$

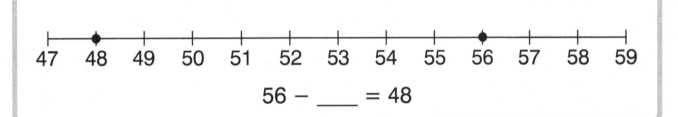

$$56 - \_\_\_ = 48$$

☐ Find the missing number by using a number line.

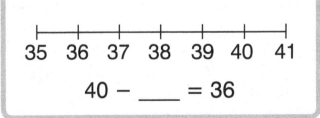

$$40 - \_\_\_ = 36$$

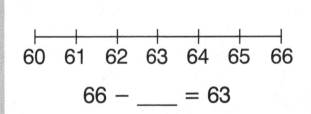

$$66 - \_\_\_ = 63$$

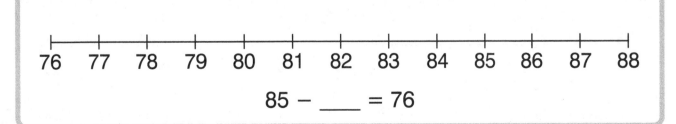

$$85 - \_\_\_ = 76$$

NS2-23 **Subtracting with a Number Line** (continued)

☐ Use a number line to add or subtract.

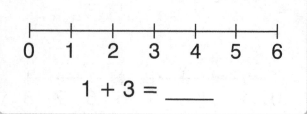

$1 + 3 = \underline{\quad}$

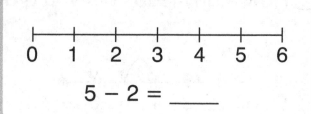

$5 - 2 = \underline{\quad}$

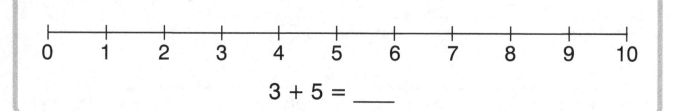

$3 + 5 = \underline{\quad}$

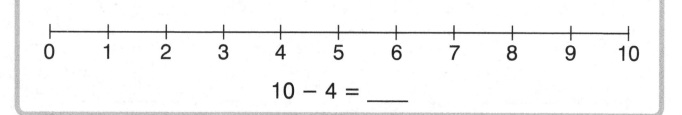

$10 - 4 = \underline{\quad}$

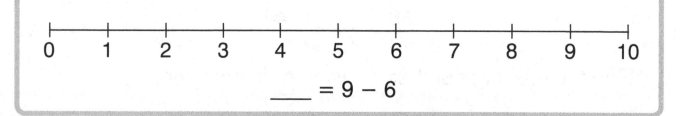

$\underline{\quad} = 9 - 6$

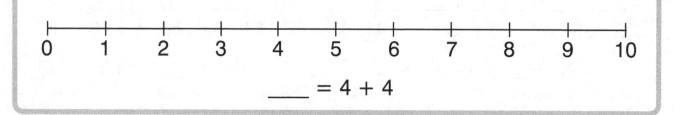

$\underline{\quad} = 4 + 4$

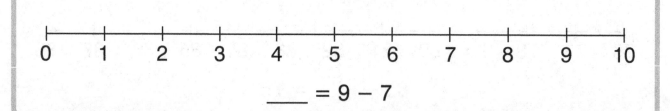

$\underline{\quad} = 9 - 7$

NS2-24 **Subtracting by Counting Backwards**

☐ Subtract by counting back.

8   _7_   _6_   _5_   _4_   _3_   8 − 5 = _3_

6   __   __   __   __   6 − 4 = ___

28   __   __   __   28 − 3 = ___

32   __   __   __   __   __   32 − 5 = ___

☐ Now draw the blanks, then subtract.

21   __   __   __   __   __   21 − 2 = ___

30   __   __   __   __   __   30 − 5 = ___

43   __   __   __   __   __   43 − 4 = ___

☐ Now keep track on your fingers.

28 − 4 = ___   32 − 3 = ___   41 − 2 = ___

NS2-25 Comparing Number Sentences

☐ Fill in the blanks.

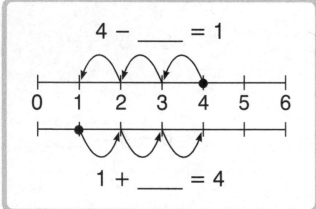

$$4 - \underline{\hphantom{00}} = 1$$

$$1 + \underline{\hphantom{00}} = 4$$

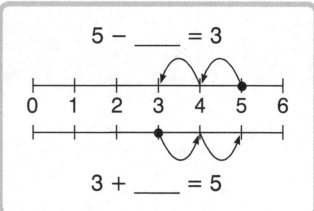

$$5 - \underline{\hphantom{00}} = 3$$

$$3 + \underline{\hphantom{00}} = 5$$

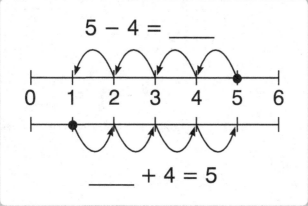

$$5 - 4 = \underline{\hphantom{00}}$$

$$\underline{\hphantom{00}} + 4 = 5$$

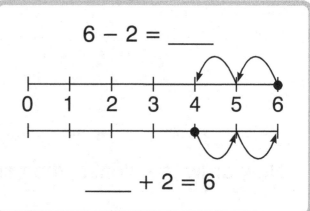

$$6 - 2 = \underline{\hphantom{00}}$$

$$\underline{\hphantom{00}} + 2 = 6$$

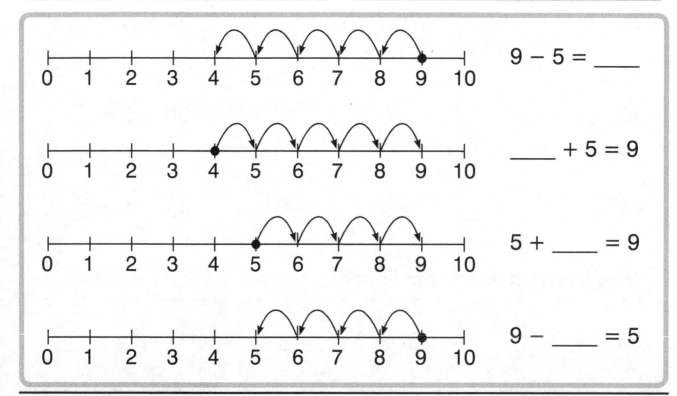

$$9 - 5 = \underline{\hphantom{00}}$$

$$\underline{\hphantom{00}} + 5 = 9$$

$$5 + \underline{\hphantom{00}} = 9$$

$$9 - \underline{\hphantom{00}} = 5$$

NS2-26 **Subtracting by Counting On**

☐ Subtract by counting forwards.

What is 31 − 27?

27   28   29   30   31

27 + __4__ = 31   so   31 − 27 = __4__

6 + __ = 8 so 8 − 6 = __

36 + __ = 38 so 38 − 36 = __

9 + __ = 12 so 12 − 9 = __

39 + __ = 42 so 42 − __ = 39

14 + __ = 19 so 19 − 14 = __

44 + __ = 49 so 49 − 44 = __

24 − 18 = __

52 − 49 = __

78 − 77 = __

89 − 86 = __

92 − 88 = __

93 − 89 = __

94 − 90 = __

95 − 91 = __

☐ Make up 3 subtraction questions and solve them by counting forwards.

NS2-26 Subtracting by Counting On (continued)

☐ Subtract by counting forwards or backwards.

47 − 4 = ____	39 − 36 = ____	42 − 38 = ____
31 − 6 = ____	32 − 25 = ____	33 − 29 = ____
33 − 4 = ____	45 − 7 = ____	41 − 39 = ____
21 − 15 = ____	21 − 3 = ____	46 − 8 = ____
42 − 36 = ____	42 − 5 = ____	37 − 35 = ____
24 − 3 = ____	24 − 19 = ____	37 − 4 = ____
47 − 5 = ____	47 − 2 = ____	47 − 43 = ____

☐ Did you use counting forwards or backwards for the last question? Explain your choice.

☐ Make up 3 subtraction questions and solve them by counting backwards.

NS2-27 **Subtracting in Word Problems**

☐ Subtract by counting forwards.
☐ Write a sentence to describe how many **more**.

Sara has 12 marbles.
Ron has 8 marbles.

Sara has 4 more marbles than Ron.

Sara has 7 apples.
Sara has 9 oranges.

Ron has 8 crayons.
Ron has 5 markers.

Sara has 6 crayons.
Ron has 10 crayons.

NS2-27 Subtracting in Word Problems (continued)

☐ Circle the correct way to answer the question.
☐ Write the answer.

Isobel had five bananas.
She ate three bananas.

5 + 3   (5 – 3)

How many bananas are **left**? __2__

There are eight big pencils.
There are five little pencils.

8 + 5   8 – 5

How many pencils **altogether**? _____

There are eight big pencils.
There are five little pencils.

8 + 5   8 – 5

How many **more** big pencils **than** little pencils? _____

There are fourteen red balloons.
There are three blue balloons.

14 + 3   14 – 3

How many **more** red balloons **than** blue ballons? _____

There are fourteen red balloons.
There are three blue balloons.

14 + 3   14 – 3

How many balloons **in total**? _____

Sonia has eleven crayons.
Seven of them are red.

11 + 7   11 – 7

How many are **not** red? _____

NS2-28 Missing Numbers in Word Problems

☐ Write the number sentence for the story.

There are ■ red marbles.

There are 5 blue marbles.

There are 9 marbles altogether.

$$\begin{array}{r} \blacksquare \\ +5 \\ \hline 9 \end{array}$$

These are 7 red marbles.

These are 3 blue marbles.

These are ■ marbles altogether.

There are 4 red marbles.

There are ■ blue marbles.

There are 6 marbles altogether.

There are 5 red marbles.

There are ■ blue marbles.

There are 8 marbles altogether.

There are ■ red marbles.

There are 2 blue marbles.

There are 7 marbles altogether.

NS2-28 Missing Numbers in Word Problems (continued)

☐ Write the number sentence for the story.

There were ■ flies.

The frog ate 3 of them.   ■

There are 6 flies left.   − 3
                                          ─────
                                            6

There were 8 flies.

The frog ate ■ of them.

There are 5 flies left.

There were 7 flies.

The frog ate 4 of them.

There are ■ flies left.

There were 9 flies.

The frog ate ■ of them.

There are 4 flies left.

There were ■ flies.

The frog ate 2 of them.

There are 5 flies left.

NS2-28 **Missing Numbers in Word Problems** (continued)

☐ Match the number sentence to the story.
☐ Fill in the missing number.

There were 8 carrots.
Rosa ate ■ of them.
There are 5 carrots left.

$7 - 5 = \square$

Ali ate ■ carrots.
Jacob ate 2 carrots.
Altogether they ate 6 carrots.

$8 - \square = 5$

There were ■ carrots.
Ron ate 3 of them.
There are 4 carrots left.

$3 + \square = 6$

There were 7 carrots.
Nomi ate 5 of them.
There are ■ left.

$\square + 2 = 6$

Bilal ate 3 carrots.
Nomi ate ■ carrots.
Together, they ate 6 carrots.

$\square - 3 = 4$

No unauthorized copying   **Number Sense 1**

NS2-29 Making 10

☐ Hold up the correct number of fingers.

How many fingers are not up?

$10 = 7 + \underline{\textbf{3}}$

$10 = 3 + \underline{}$

$10 = 4 + \underline{}$

$10 = 5 + \underline{}$

$$\begin{array}{r} 9 \\ + \boxed{} \\ \hline 10 \end{array}$$

$$\begin{array}{r} 1 \\ + \boxed{} \\ \hline 10 \end{array}$$

$$\begin{array}{r} 2 \\ + \boxed{} \\ \hline 10 \end{array}$$

$$\begin{array}{r} 10 \\ + \boxed{} \\ \hline 10 \end{array}$$

$10 - 8 = \underline{}$

$10 - 6 = \underline{}$

$10 - 5 = \underline{}$

$10 - 9 = \underline{}$

NS2-29 Making 10 (continued)

☐ Circle the number that makes 10 with the number in bold.

8
1
②
3
4
5

6
1
2
3
4
5

7
1
2
3
4
5

5
1
2
3
4
5

9
1
2
3
4
5

4
6　9
7　8

1
6　9
7　8

3
6　9
7　8

2
9　6
8　5
7　4

☐ Circle the two numbers that make 10.

4	5	6

3	7	9

4	5	5

1	2	3	9

4	5	6	7

2	4	6	9

1	9	3	5

2	4	3	8

2	3	7	9

1	2	6	7	8

2	3	4	7	9

1	3	4	8	9

2	3	6	8	9

2	3	4	5	6

3	5	6	7	8

NS2-30 Adding 10 and Subtracting 10

☐ Circle the next 10 numbers.
☐ Add 10.

1	2	3	4	5	6	7	8	9	10
11	12	13	14	15	16	17	18	19	20

4 + 10 = ___

11	12	13	14	15	16	17	18	19	20
21	22	23	24	25	26	27	28	29	30

19 + 10 = ___

31	32	33	34	35	36	37	38	39	40
41	42	43	44	45	46	47	48	49	50

38 + 10 = ___

81	82	83	84	85	86	87	88	89	90
91	92	93	94	95	96	97	98	99	100

90 + 10 = ___

☐ Add 10 by moving down a row.

1	2	3	4	5	6	7	8	9	10
11	12	13	14	15	16	17	18	19	20

3 + 10 = ___

7 + 10 = ___

9 + 10 = ___

NS2-30 Adding 10 and Subtracting 10 (continued)

☐ Circle the previous 10 numbers.
☐ Subtract 10.

1	2	3	4	5	6	⑦	⑧	⑨	⑩
⑪	⑫	⑬	⑭	⑮	⑯	**17**	18	19	20

17 – 10 = ____

11	12	13	14	15	16	17	18	19	20
21	22	23	24	25	26	27	28	29	**30**

30 – 10 = ____

41	42	43	44	45	46	47	48	49	50
51	**52**	53	54	55	56	57	58	59	60

52 – 10 = ____

☐ Move up a row to subtract 10.

71	72	73	74	75	76	77	78	79	80
81	82	83	84	85	86	87	88	89	90

82 – 10 = ____

85 – 10 = ____

90 – 10 = ____

When subtracting 10, the _____ digit stays the same
                         ones/tens

and the _____ digit goes _____ by 1.
         ones/tens   up/down

☐ Subtract 10.

76 – 10 = ____   38 – 10 = ____   99 – 10 = ____

NS2-31 More Adding and Subtracting 10

☐ Circle the two numbers that make 10.
☐ Add.

⑧+②+ 5 = 10 + __5__

= __15__

4 + 6 + 7 = 10 + ___

= ___

2 + 3 + 7 = 10 + ___

= ___

1 + 6 + 4 = 10 + ___

= ___

8 + 5 + 5 = 10 + ___

= ___

7 + 6 + 3 = 10 + ___

= ___

4 + 9 + 1 = 10 + ___

= ___

8 + 3 + 2 = 10 + ___

= ___

4 + 5 + 5 = 10 + ___

= ___

2 + 9 + 8 = 10 + ___

= ___

3 + 5 + 7 = 10 + ___

= ___

1 + 8 + 9 = 10 + ___

= ___

NS2-32 Hundreds Chart Pieces

The boxes are pieces from a hundreds chart.

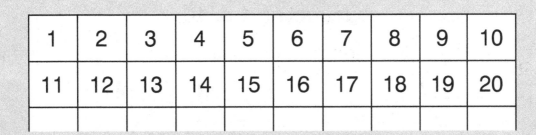

1	2	3	4	5	6	7	8	9	10
11	12	13	14	15	16	17	18	19	20

☐ Find the missing numbers by…

adding 1.

| 3 | | | 17 | | | 19 | | | 6 | |

adding 10.

| 23 | | 30 | | 6 | | 24 | | 31 | | 29 |

adding 1 or 10.

| 45 | | | 50 | | 41 | | | 52 | | 53 | | 56 | |

adding 1 then 10 or 10 then 1.

| 71 | | | 77 | | 74 | | | 86 | | 82 |

☐ Have a partner check your answers using a hundreds chart.

NS2-32 **Hundreds Chart Pieces** (continued)

☐ Find the missing numbers by...

subtracting 1 or 10.

 48   57   43   43   41   40

subtracting 1 then 10 or 10 then 1.

92   89   77   85   90

adding or subtracting 1 or 10.

26   37   39   39   39   39

adding or subtracting or both.

18   24   17   38   15

 35   19   46   18   47

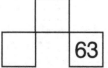 63   74

   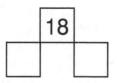 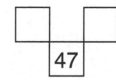

☐ Have a partner check your answers using a hundreds chart.

NS2-32 **Hundreds Chart Pieces** (continued)

☐ Write the missing numbers on the hundreds chart pieces.

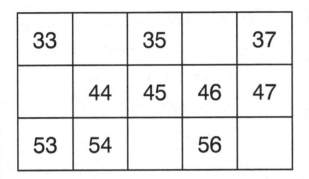

33		35		37
	44	45	46	47
53	54		56	

11	12	13	
21		23	24
	32	33	

61	62	
71		73
		83
91	92	

64		66
	75	
	85	
94		96

	49
58	
	69
78	

46				50
	57		59	
		68		
	77		79	
86				90

	57	58	59	60
66				
	77			
		88		
			99	100

NS2-33 Problems and Puzzles

A
Aza had 7 kittens.
She gave 4 to friends.
How many kittens does
she have left?

A = _____

T
Tara had three pencils.
She bought seven more.
How many does
she have now?

T = _____

H
Hew has seventeen
hockey cards and
three baseball cards.
How many cards does
he have altogether?

H = _____

M
Maria did 11 jumping jacks.
Michael did 9 jumping jacks.
How many more
jumping jacks did Maria
do than Michael?

M = _____

Write your answers in order from smallest to largest.

Numbers: _____ _____ _____ _____

Their letters: _____ _____ _____ _____

Solve the number crossword.

ACROSS

1. 84 − 10

2. 8 + 8

1	2
2	

DOWN

1. 70 + 1

2. 36 + 10

Use your "down" answers to check your "across" answers.

How many dots are on a die ? _____

UNIT 2

Patterns and Algebra 1

PA2-1 Finding the Core and Extending Patterns

The parts that repeat are the **core**.
Each part is a **term**.

☐ Circle the core.

PA2-2 What Changes?

Which **attribute** changes?

3 Ɛ 3 Ɛ

size   ~~direction~~ (circled)

shape   direction

b c b c b c

shape   direction

b d b d b d

colour   direction

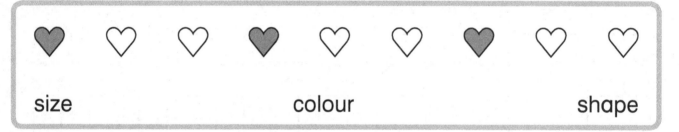

size   colour   shape

B B B B B B B B B B B B

direction   shape   size   colour

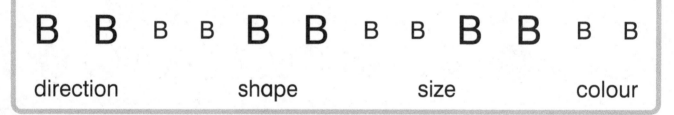

direction   shape   size   thickness

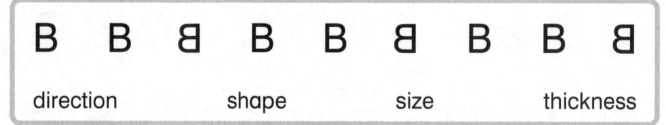

direction   shape   size   thickness

PA2-2 **What Changes?** *(continued)*

☐ **What changes? Choose two.**

direction	size	shape	colour	thickness

3 & 3 & 3 &

_____ *direction* _____ and _____ *thickness* _____

○ ○ ★ ○ ○ ★ ○ ○ ★

_____ and _____

○ ● ○ ○ ● ○ ○ ● ○

_____ and _____

⇒ ⇒ ⇐ ⇐ ⇒ ⇒ ⇐ ⇐

_____ and _____

b d d b d d b d d

_____ and _____

PA2-2 **What Changes?** *(continued)*

☐ Circle the core.
☐ Draw the next three terms.

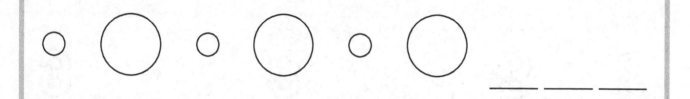

_____ _____ _____ _____

_____ _____ _____ _____

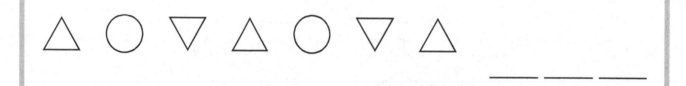

_____ _____ _____ _____

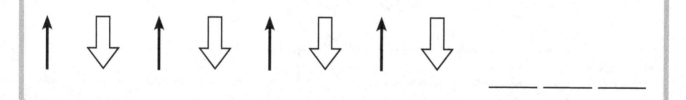

_____ _____ _____ _____

2 2 **2** **2** 2 **2**

_____ _____ _____ _____

A A B A A B

_____ _____ _____ _____

PA2-2 What Changes? *(continued)*

⬜ Create a pattern where...

only **colour** changes.

only **size** changes.

only **shape** changes.

colour and **size** change.

colour and **shape** change.

📓 Create a pattern where two things change. What changes?

PA2-3 Cores that End the Way They Start

☐ Circle the core.

○ ☆ ○   ○ ☆ ○   ○ ☆ ○   ○ ☆ ○

● ○ ●   ● ○ ●   ● ○ ●   ● ○ ●

1 2 1 1 2 1 1 2 1 1 2 1 1 2 1

2 3 4 2 2 3 4 2 2 3 4 2

1 2 3 2 1 1 2 3 2 1 1 2 3 2 1

PA2-4 Pattern Rules

☐ Circle the core.
☐ Describe the pattern. Choose words from:

thin	thick	small	big	light	dark

3 **3** **3** **3** **3** **3** **3** **3** **3** **3** **3** **3**

___*thin*___, ___*thick*___, ___*repeat*___

_____, _____, _____, ___*repeat*___

_____, _____, _____, ___*repeat*___

_____, _____, _____, _____, ___*repeat*___

☐ Now say when to repeat as well.

_____

PA2-4 **Pattern Rules** *(continued)*

☐ Describe how **two** attributes change.

A ∀ ∀ A ∀ ∀ A ∀ ∀

Size: ___***big***___ , ___***small***___ , ___***small***___ , ___***repeat***___

Direction: ___***up***___ , _____ , _____ , _____

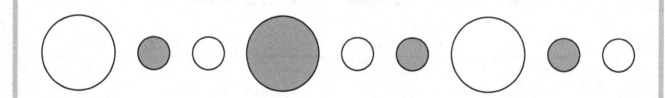

Size: _____ , _____ , _____ , ___***repeat***___

Colour: _____ , _____ , _____

Shape: _____ , _____ , _____ , ___***repeat***___

Thickness: _____ , _____ , _____ , _____

PA2-5 Showing Patterns in Different Ways

☐ Use letters to show the pattern.
   Put the same letter under the same figures.

A   B   B   A   B   B

_____ _____ _____ _____ _____ _____

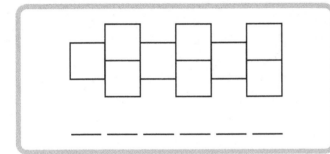

_____ _____ _____ _____ _____ _____

7   0   9   7   0   9

_____ _____ _____ _____ _____ _____

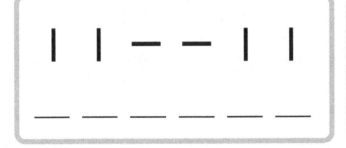

_____ _____ _____ _____ _____ _____

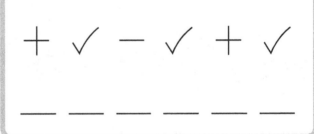

_____ _____ _____ _____ _____ _____

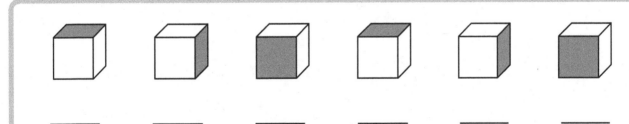

_____ _____ _____ _____ _____ _____

_____ _____ _____ _____ _____ _____ _____ _____ _____ _____ _____ _____

No unauthorized copying

UNIT 3

Measurement 1

ME2-1 **Measuring Length**

Use big .

How many long?

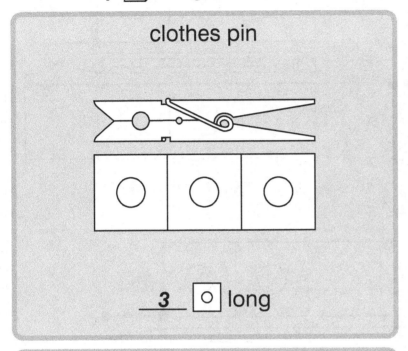

clothes pin

_3_ ⊡ long

needle

____ ⊡ long

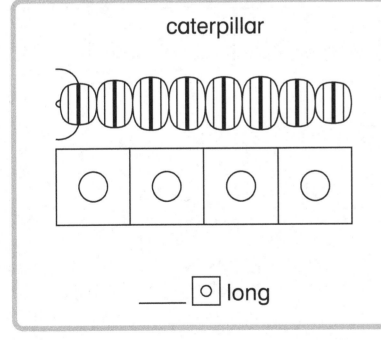

caterpillar

____ ⊡ long

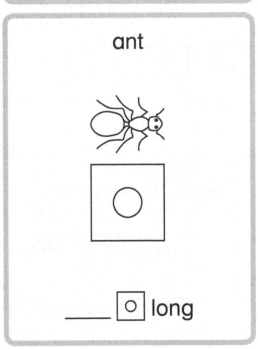

ant

____ ⊡ long

☐ Order the needle, ant, and caterpillar from shortest to longest.

_____   _____   _____

shortest   longest

ME2-1 **Measuring Length** *(continued)*

⬭ The length is closer to…

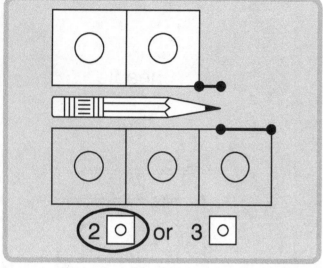

2 ☐ or 3 ☐

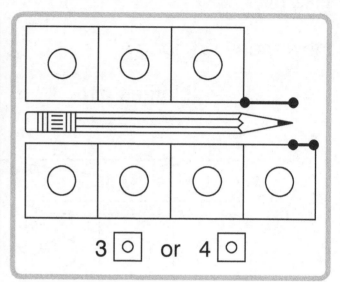

3 ☐ or 4 ☐

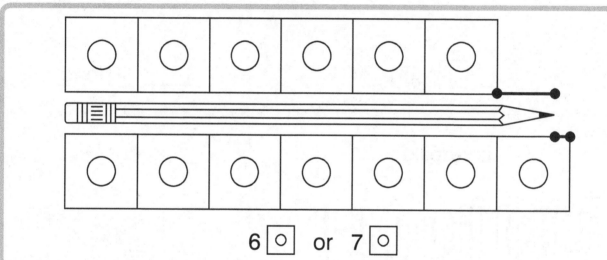

6 ☐ or 7 ☐

⬭ Measure with big ⬜.

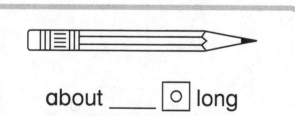

about _____ ☐ long

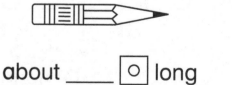

about _____ ☐ long

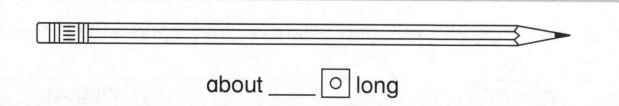

about _____ ☐ long

ME2-2 How to Measure

☐ Explain what is wrong with each measurement.

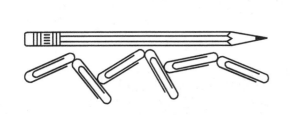

6 ⌒ long

_____

_____

_____

_____

5 ☐ long

_____

_____

_____

_____

5 ⌒ long

_____

_____

_____

_____

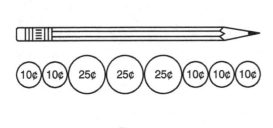

8 (10¢) long

_____

_____

_____

_____

ME2-3 **Comparing Units**

- ☐ Measure two ways.
- ☐ Write which way needed more and why.

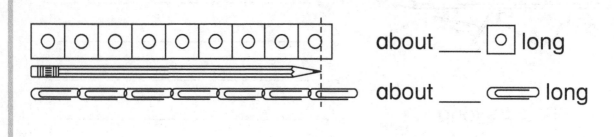

about ____ ⬜ long

about ____ ⬭ long

I used _____ more / fewer _____ ☐ than ⬭

because a ☐ is _____ longer / shorter _____ than a ⬭.

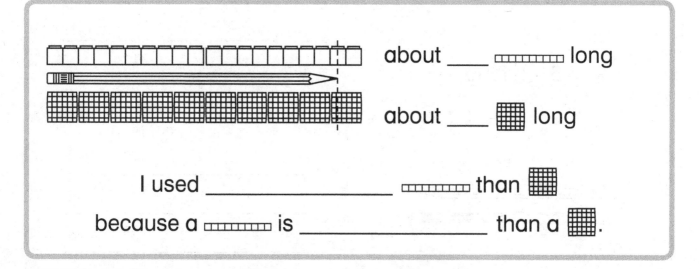

about ____ ▭▭▭ long

about ____ ▦ long

I used _____ ▭▭▭ than ▦

because a ▭▭▭ is _____ than a ▦.

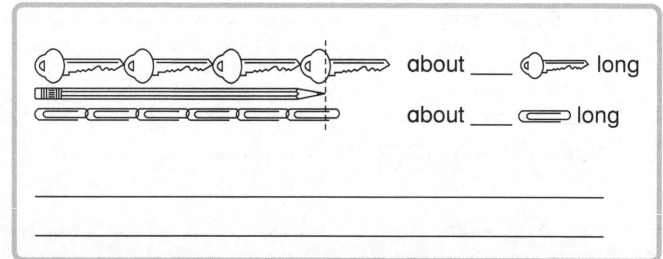

about ____ ⚷ long

about ____ ⬭ long

_____

_____

ME2-4 **Centimetres**

A small 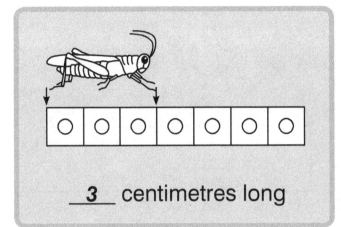 is 1 centimetre long.

☐ Write how many centimetres long.

___3___ centimetres long

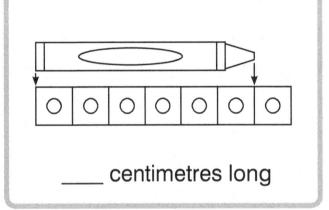

____ centimetres long

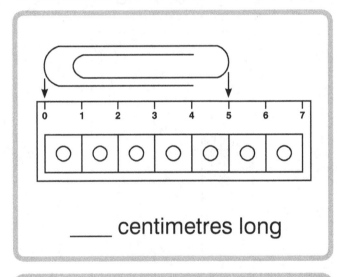

____ centimetres long

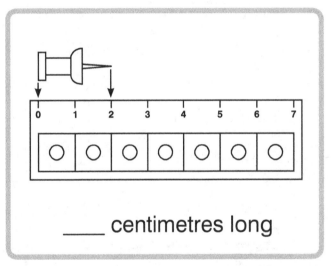

____ centimetres long

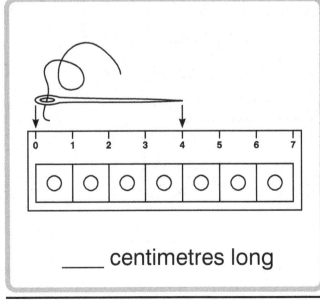

____ centimetres long

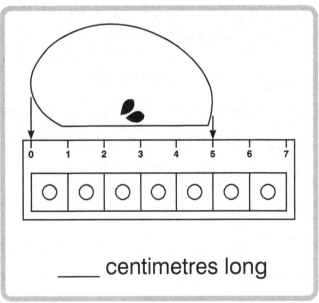

____ centimetres long

ME2-4 **Centimetres** (continued)

We write **cm** for **c**enti**m**etre.

☐ Fill in the blanks.

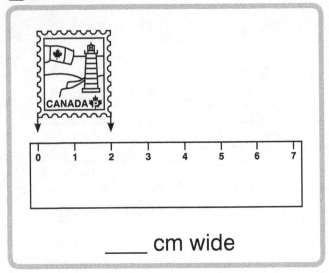

_____ cm wide

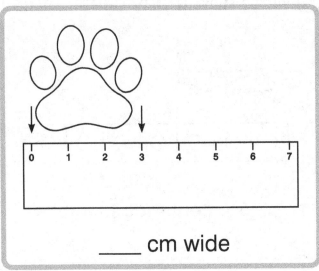

_____ cm wide

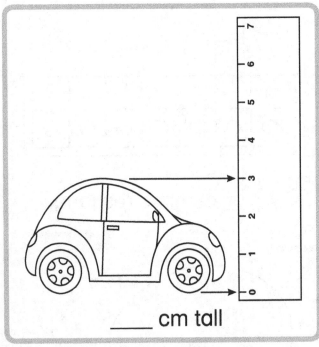

_____ cm tall

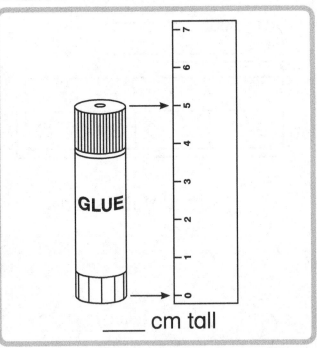

_____ cm tall

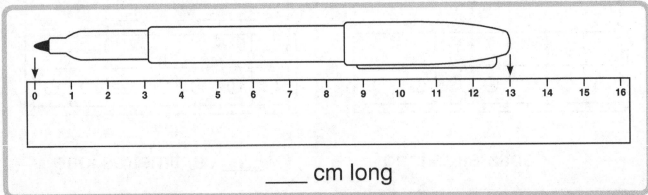

_____ cm long

ME2-4 **Centimetres** (continued)

☐ Measure the pictures.

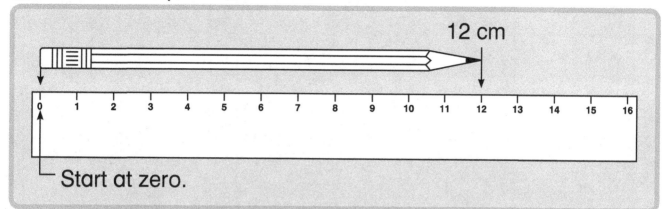

12 cm

Start at zero.

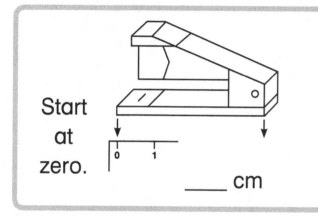

Start at zero.

_____ cm

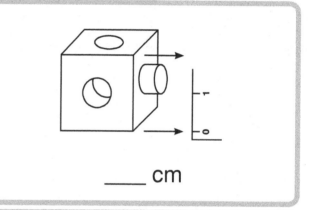

_____ cm

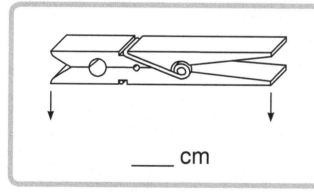

_____ cm

Start at both places.

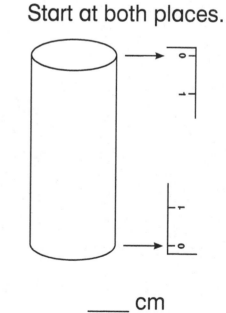

_____ cm

☐ Did you get the same answer? Explain why.

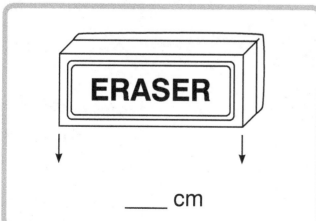

ERASER

_____ cm

UNIT 4

Probability and Data Management 1

PDM2-1 **Sorting into Groups**

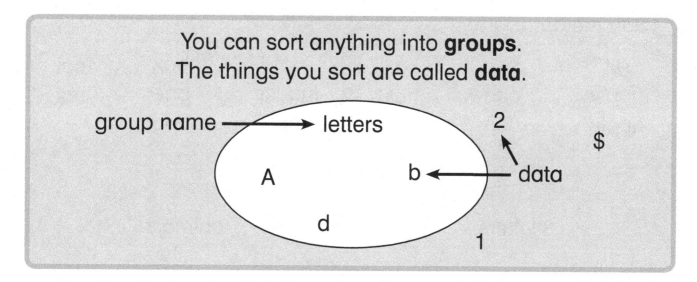

You can sort anything into **groups**.
The things you sort are called **data**.

group name ⟶ letters

2

$

A   b ← data

d

1

☐ Sort the data.

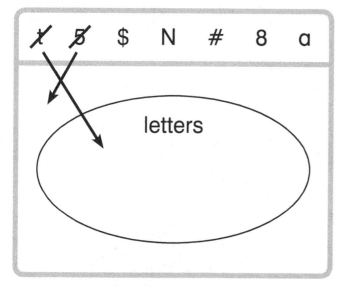

X̸   5̸ $ N   #   8   a

letters

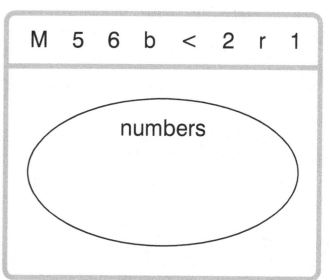

M   5   6   b   <   2   r   1

numbers

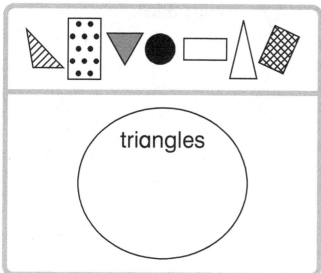

triangles

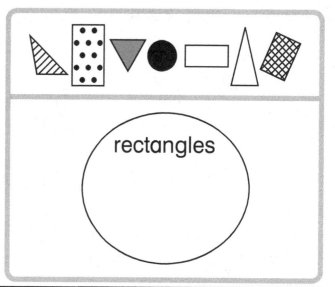

rectangles

PDM2-1 **Sorting into Groups** (continued)

☐ Sort the data.

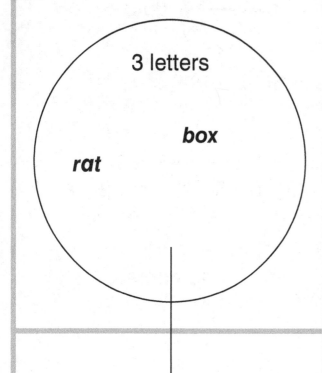

rat	box	cat
mouse	one	hat
apple	dog	

3 letters

box

rat

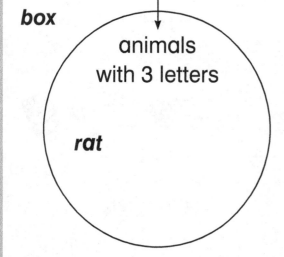

box

animals
with 3 letters

rat

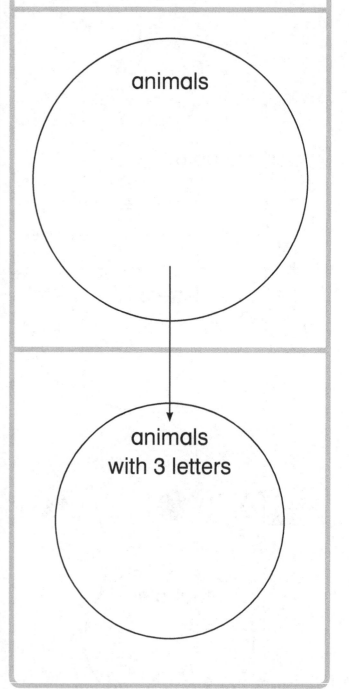

rat	box	cat
mouse	one	hat
apple	dog	

animals

animals
with 3 letters

☐ Did you get the same answer? _____

PDM2-2 **Sorting Rules**

☐ Find one word that describes the data.

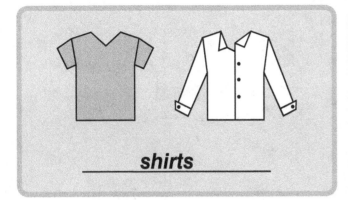

___shirts___

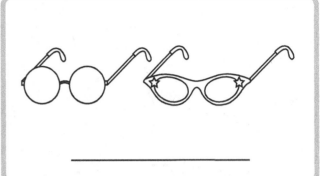

_____

_____

_____

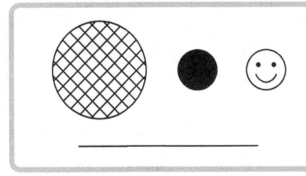

_____

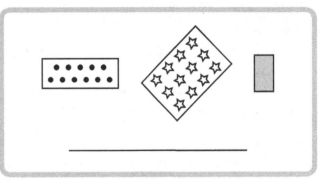

_____

☐ Find two words that describe the data.

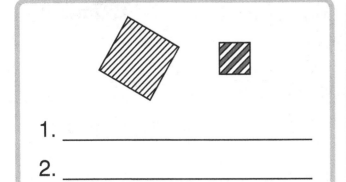

1. _____

2. _____

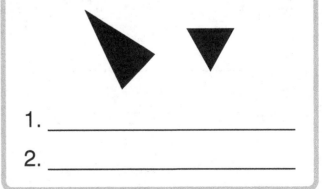

1. _____

2. _____

PDM2-2 **Sorting Rules** (continued)

☐ How were these sorted? Write two properties.

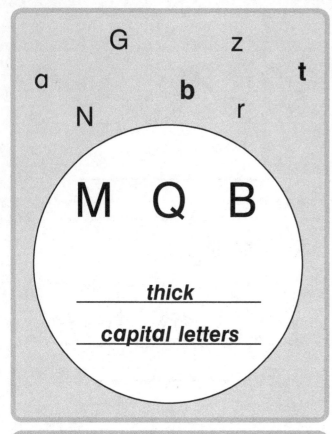

thick

capital letters

_____

_____

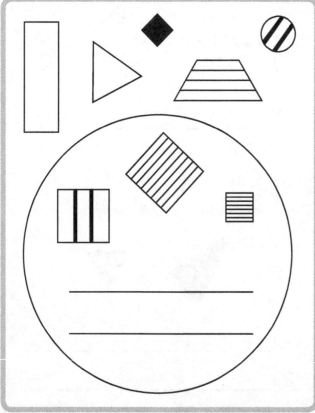

_____

_____

_____

_____

PDM2-3 Sort and Graph

☐ Sort the data.
☐ Write the sorted data in the correct rows.

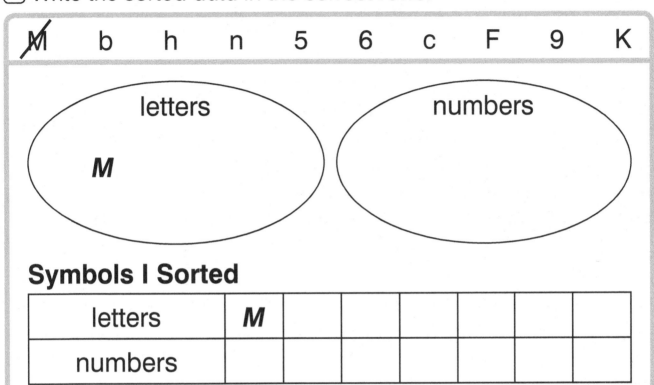

M   b   h   n   5   6   c   F   9   K

letters   numbers

M

Symbols I Sorted

letters	*M*						
numbers							

am   bat   sit   on   two   or   day

3 letters   2 letters

Words in My List

3 letters				
2 letters				

UNIT 5

Number Sense 2

NS2-34 Skip Counting

Count by 2s and colour the numbers that you say.

☐ Start at **2** and colour the numbers **blue**.

☐ Start at **1** and colour the numbers **red**.

1	2	3	4	5	6	7	8	9	10
11	12	13	14	15	16	17	18	19	20
21	22	23	24	25	26	27	28	29	30
31	32	33	34	35	36	37	38	39	40

The blue numbers have ones digit ___, ___, ___, ___, or ___.

The red numbers have ones digit ___, ___, ___, ___, or ___.

☐ Count by 2s.

2, _____, _____, _____, _____, _____, _14_

42, _____, _____, _____, _____, _____, _____

86, _____, _____, _____, _94_, _____, _____

1, _____, _____, _____, _9_, _____, _____

61, _____, _____, _____, _____, _____, _____

☐ Count back by 2s.

86, _84_, _____, _____, _____, _76_, _____

NS2-34 **Skip Counting** (continued)

☐ Start at 5 and count by 5s. Colour the numbers that you say.

1	2	3	4	5	6	7	8	9	10
11	12	13	14	15	16	17	18	19	20
21	22	23	24	25	26	27	28	29	30

The coloured numbers have ones digit ＿＿ or ＿＿.

☐ Count by 5s.

0 ___5___ _____ _____ _____ _____ _____ _____

60 ___65___ _____ _____ _____ _____ _____ _____

70 _____ _____ _____ _____ ___95___ _____

☐ Count back by 5s.

30 ___25___ _____ _____ _____ _____ _____

80 _____ _____ _____ _____ ___55___ _____

100 _____ _____ ___85___ _____ _____ _____

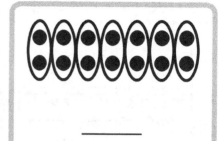

NS2-34 **Skip Counting** *(continued)*

☐ Count by 2s and then by 1s to see how many.

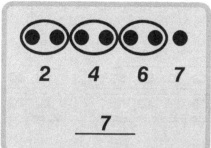

2   4   6   7

_____7_____

_____

_____

☐ Count by 5s and then by 1s to see how many.

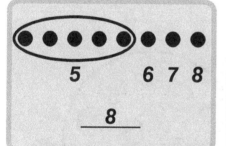

5   6 7 8

_____8_____

_____

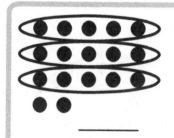

_____

      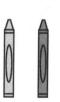

_____

There are _____ letters in the alphabet.

NS2-34 **Skip Counting** *(continued)*

☐ Count how many.
Use groups of 10.

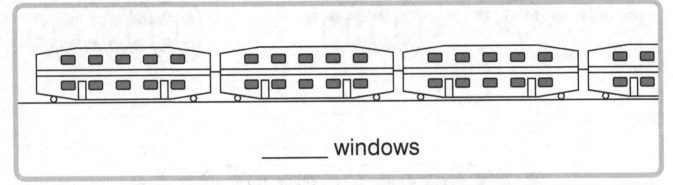

_____ windows

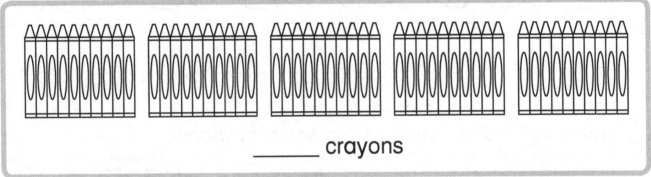

_____ crayons

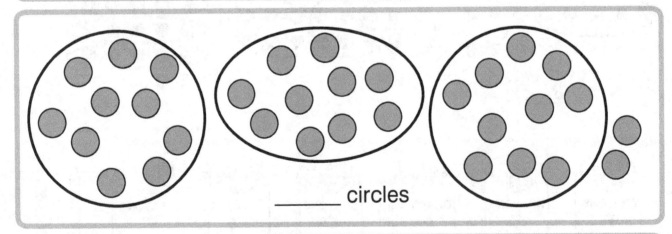

_____ circles

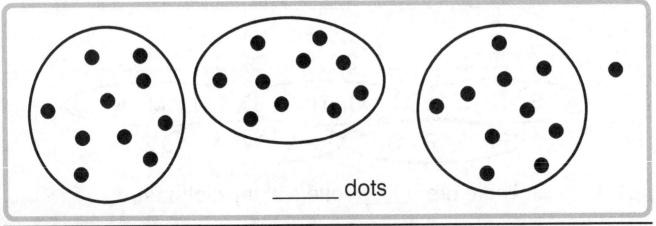

_____ dots

No unauthorized copying

NS2-34 Skip Counting (continued)

Count by 10s and colour the numbers that you say.

◯ Start at **10** and colour the numbers **red**.

◯ Start at **7** and colour the numbers **blue**.

1	2	3	4	5	6	7	8	9	10
11	12	13	14	15	16	17	18	19	20
21	22	23	24	25	26	27	28	29	30
31	32	33	34	35	36	37	38	39	40

The red numbers have ones digit _____.

The blue numbers have ones digit _____.

◯ Count by 10s.

20 _____ _____ **50** _____ _____ _____

40 _____ _____ _____ _____ **90** _____

37 _____ _____ _____ **77** _____ _____

22 _____ _____ _____ _____ _____ _____

15 _____ _____ _____ _____ _____ _____

NS2-35 Estimating Numbers

10 dots are circled.

☐ Estimate the closest ten. _____
☐ Circle 2 more groups of 10. Estimate again. _____

☐ Group by 10s to count. _____
Did circling more groups of 10 improve your estimate? yes / no
☐ Why do you think that happened?

NS2-36 Adding Tens and Ones

Write the number as a sum of 10s and 1s.

32 = **10 + 10 + 10 + 1 + 1**	13 =
41 =	22 =

We can write 24 = 20 + 4. Write each number in the same way.

35 = **30 + 5**	47 = _____	63 = _____
81 = _____	56 = _____	92 = _____

Add.

40 + 5 = **45**	6 + 20 = ____	70 + 1 = ____
8 + 60 = ____	70 + 7 = ____	4 + 50 = ____
30 + 8 = ____	9 + 10 = ____	6 + 80 = ____
7 + 90 = ____	9 + 70 = ____	70 + 9 = ____

NS2-36 **Adding Tens and Ones** (continued)

⬜ Add.

5 + 2 = 1 + 1 + 1 + 1 + 1 + 1 + 1 = _____

50 + 20 = 10 + 10 + 10 + 10 + 10 + 10 + 10 = _____

4 + 4 = 1 + 1 + 1 + 1 + 1 + 1 + 1 + 1 = _____

40 + 40 = 10 + 10 + 10 + 10 + 10 + 10 + 10 + 10 = _____

2 + 3 = 1 + 1 + 1 + 1 + 1 = _____

20 + 30 = 10 + 10 + 10 + 10 + 10 = _____

2 + 6 = _____

20 + 60 = _____

4 + 1 = _____

40 + 10 = _____

5 + 4 = _____

50 + 40 = _____

1 + 5 = _____

10 + 50 = _____

3 + 3 = _____

30 + 30 = _____

3 + 4 = _____

30 + 40 = _____

1 + 3 + 2 = _____

10 + 30 + 20 = _____

2 + 3 + 2 + 1 = _____

20 + 30 + 20 + 10 = _____

NS2-37 **Adding in Two Ways**

☐ Separate the dots in two different places.
☐ Write an addition sentence.

___3___ + ___6___ = ___5___ + ___4___

_____ + _____ = _____ + _____

_____ + _____ = _____ + _____

_____ + _____ = _____ + _____

_____

_____

NS2-38 Addition Strategies

◯ Move the line one place to the right ⟶.
◯ Write the new addition sentence.

● ● | ● ● ● ●   2 + 4 = 6

● ● ● ● | ● ● ●   *3 + 3 = 6*

● | ● ● ● ●   1 + 4 = 5

● ● ● ● ●

● ● ● | ● ● ●   3 + 2 = 5

● ● ● ● ●

● ● ● ● | ● ●   4 + 2 = 6

● ● ● ● ● ● ●

● ● | ● ●   2 + 2 = 4

● ● ● ●

● | ● ●   1 + 2 = 3

● ● ●

| ● ● ● ●   0 + 4 = 4

● ● ● ●

● ● ● | ●   3 + 1 = 4

● ● ● ●

How does the first number change? _____ *It goes up by 1.* _____

How does the second number change? _____

What happens to the total? _____

⧘◻ Why does that happen?

NS2-38 Addition Strategies *(continued)*

☐ Add and subtract 1 to make a new number sentence.

2 + 5 = 7
[+1] [−1]
[3] + [4] = [7]

3 + 8 = 11
[+1] [−1]
☐ + ☐ = ☐

6 + 3 = 9
[+1] [−1]
☐ + ☐ = ☐

8 + 3 = 11
[+1] [−1]
☐ + ☐ = ☐

5 + 9 = 14
☐ ☐
☐ + ☐ = ☐

5 + 2 = 7
☐ ☐
☐ + ☐ = ☐

7 + 11 = 18
☐ ☐
☐ + ☐ = ☐

11 + 7 = 18
☐ ☐
☐ + ☐ = ☐

☐ Finish the addition sentence.

6 + 11 = 7 + _____

8 + 4 = 9 + _____

NS2-38 Addition Strategies *(continued)*

first number   second number

• | • • • • •   1 + 5 = 6

• • • • | • •   4 + 2 = 6

The first number went _____ ***up*** _____ by __*3*__.

The second number went _____ ***down*** _____ by __*3*__.

• • | • • • •   2 + 5 = 7

• • • • | • • •   4 + 3 = 7

The first number went _____ by _____.

The second number went _____ by _____.

• • • • • | • •   5 + 2 = 7

• | • • • • • •   1 + 6 = 7

The first number went _____ by _____.

The second number went _____ by _____.

NS2-38 Addition Strategies *(continued)*

☐ Change both numbers in opposite ways.
☐ Write the addition sentences.
☐ Did the total change?

3
$+$ [2]
___
[5]

4
$-$ [2]
___
[2]

$3 + 4 =$ __7__

__5__ $+$ __2__ $=$ __7__

Did the total change? **No**

6
$-$ [3]
___
[ ]

4
$+$ [ ]
___
[ ]

$6 + 4 =$ ____

____ $+$ ____ $=$ ____

Did the total change? ____

0
$+$ [4]
___
[ ]

9
$-$ [ ]
___
[ ]

$0 + 9 =$ ____

____ $+$ ____ $=$ ____

Did the total change? ____

6
$-$ [2]
___
[ ]

2
$+$ [ ]
___
[ ]

$6 + 2 =$ ____

____ $+$ ____ $=$ ____

Did the total change? ____

NS2-39 **Using 10 to Add**

☐ Circle a group of 10.
☐ Use 10 to add.

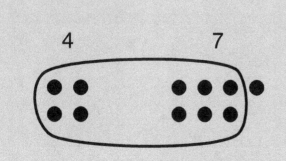

4 + 7 = 10 + __*1*__ = __*11*__

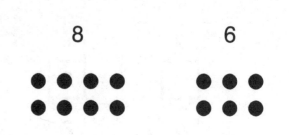

8 + 6 = 10 + _____ = _____

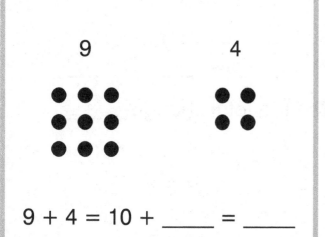

9 + 4 = 10 + _____ = _____

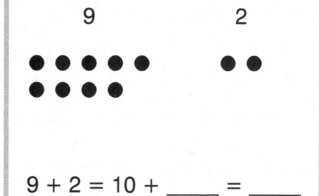

9 + 2 = 10 + _____ = _____

7

7

7 + 7 = 10 + _____ = _____

Make your own.

NS2-39 **Using 10 to Add** (continued)

☐ What makes 10 with the first number?
  Subtract that amount from the second number.

☐ Use 10 to add.

first number   second number
        ↓   ↓
        8   5

$+ \boxed{2}$ $- \boxed{2}$

   10            $\boxed{3}$

$8 + 5 = 10 + \underline{\ 3\ } = \underline{\ 13\ }$

8   7

$+\ \square$ $-\ \square$

10          $\square$

$8 + 7 = 10 + \underline{\ \ \ } = \underline{\ \ \ }$

8   8

$+\ \square$ $-\ \square$

10          $\square$

$8 + 8 = 10 + \underline{\ \ \ } = \underline{\ \ \ }$

9   3

$+\ \square$ $-\ \square$

10          $\square$

$9 + 3 = 10 + \underline{\ \ \ } = \underline{\ \ \ }$

3   9

$+\ \square$ $-\ \square$

10          $\square$

$3 + 9 = 10 + \underline{\ \ \ } = \underline{\ \ \ }$

8   6

$+\ \square$ $-\ \square$

10          $\square$

$8 + 6 = 10 + \underline{\ \ \ } = \underline{\ \ \ }$

☐ Which two questions have the same answer?
  Why did that happen?
  Which question was easier?

NS2-40 Using Tens and Ones to Add

How many tens and ones altogether?

◯ Add.

<u> 2 </u> tens + <u> 5 </u> ones

13   +   12   =   <u> 25 </u>

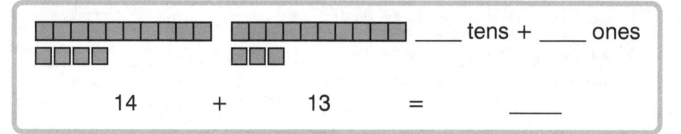

____ tens + ____ ones

14   +   13   =   ____

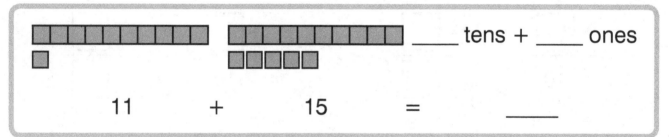

____ tens + ____ ones

11   +   15   =   ____

◯ Now draw the blocks and add.

____ tens + ____ ones

12   +   12   =   ____

◯ Make your own problem.

____ tens + ____ ones

=   ____

NS2-40 Using Tens and Ones to Add (continued)

☐ Add by separating the tens and ones.

23	=	20 + 3	
+ 34	=	30 + 4	
57 ←		50 + 7	

34	=	30 + 4	
+ 15	=	10 + 5	
☐ ←		40 + 9	

27 = 20 + ☐
+ 22 = 20 + ☐
☐ ← 40 + ☐

35 = ☐ + ☐
+ 42 = ☐ + ☐
☐ ← ☐ + ☐

15 = ☐ + ☐
+ 23 = ☐ + ☐
☐ ← ☐ + ☐

26 = ☐ + ☐
+ 13 = ☐ + ☐
☐ ← ☐ + ☐

34 = ☐ + ☐
+ 54 = ☐ + ☐
☐ ← ☐ + ☐

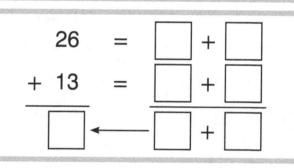

26 = ☐ + ☐
+ 33 = ☐ + ☐
☐ ← ☐ + ☐

22 = ☐ + ☐
14 = ☐ + ☐
+ 21 = ☐ + ☐
☐ ← ☐ + ☐

11 = ☐ + ☐
22 = ☐ + ☐
+ 33 = ☐ + ☐
☐ ← ☐ + ☐

NS2-40 **Using Tens and Ones to Add** *(continued)*

☐ Add by using a tens and ones chart.

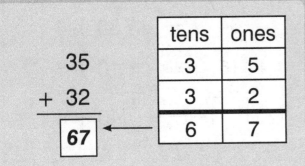

35
+ 32
67

tens	ones
3	5
3	2
6	7

24
+ 41

tens	ones
2	4
4	1

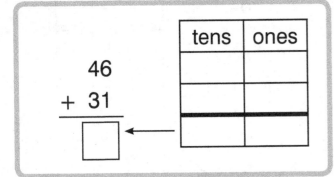

46
+ 31

tens	ones

43
+ 23

tens	ones

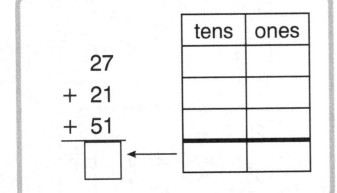

27
+ 21
+ 51

tens	ones

31
+ 42
+ 14

tens	ones

tens	ones
3	2
+ 2	7

tens	ones
4	8
+ 3	1

tens	ones
5	5
+ 2	3

tens	ones
2	2
+ 1	3

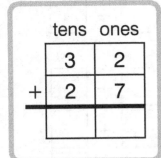

37
+ 22

63
+ 16

25
+ 34

31
+ 62

54
+ 34

23
+ 43

NS2-41 **Regrouping**

☐ Group 10 ones blocks together.
☐ Add.

7   5

$7 + 5 = 10 + \underline{\textbf{\textit{2}}} = \underline{\textbf{\textit{12}}}$

6   8

$6 + 8 = 10 + \underline{\hspace{1cm}} = \underline{\hspace{1cm}}$

5   8

$5 + 8 = 10 + \underline{\hspace{1cm}} = \underline{\hspace{1cm}}$

8   4

$8 + 4 = 10 + \underline{\hspace{1cm}} = \underline{\hspace{1cm}}$

7   7

$7 + 7 = 10 + \underline{\hspace{1cm}} = \underline{\hspace{1cm}}$

NS2-41 **Regrouping** (continued)

◯ Group 10 ones blocks together.
How many tens and ones?

◯ Add.

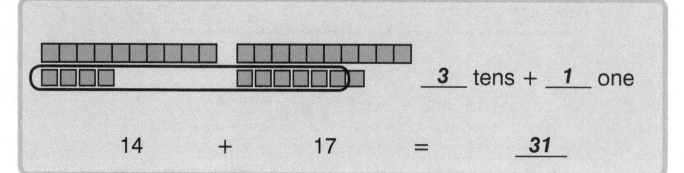

____3__ tens + ___1__ one

14   +   17   =   ___31___

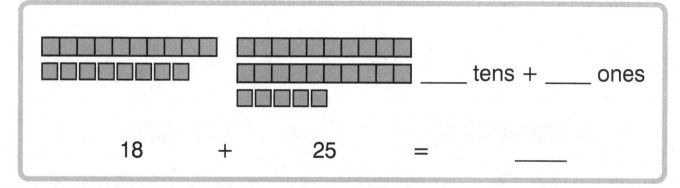

_____ tens + _____ ones

17   +   16   =   _____

_____ tens + _____ ones

18   +   25   =   _____

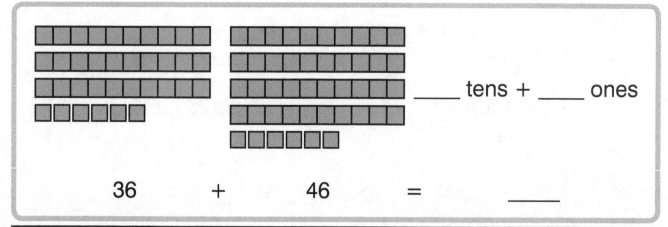

_____ tens + _____ ones

36   +   46   =   _____

NS2-41 **Regrouping** *(continued)*

☐ Trade groups of 10 ones for tens.
☐ Regroup in the next row.

tens	ones
4	27
6	**7**

tens	ones
3	12

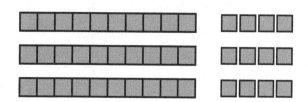

tens	ones
5	21

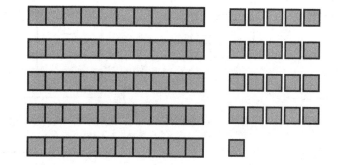

tens	ones
3	15

tens	ones
6	19

tens	ones
4	28

NS2-41 **Regrouping** (continued)

☐ Add the tens and ones.
☐ Regroup in the next row.
☐ Write the answer.

tens	ones
1	6
5	5
6	**11**
7	**1**

16
+ 55
———
71

tens	ones
1	2
2	9
4	1

12
+ 29
———
41

tens	ones
2	5
3	8
6	3

25
+ 38
———
63

tens	ones
5	7
2	6
8	3

57
+ 26
———
83

tens	ones
2	8
2	6
5	4

28
+ 26
———
54

tens	ones
2	3
5	2
1	6
9	11

23
52
+ 16
———
91

NS2-42 The Standard Algorithm for Addition

☐ Add the ones.
☐ Write the tens in the tens column.
☐ Write the ones in the ones column.

$5 + 9 = \boxed{1}\,\boxed{4}$

tens ones
$\boxed{1}$ 0
  1   5
$+$ 2   9
   4   $\boxed{4}$

$3 + 8 = \boxed{1}\,\boxed{1}$

tens ones
$\boxed{1}$
  2   3
$+$ 3   8
   6   1

$6 + 4 = \boxed{1}\,\boxed{0}$

tens ones
$\boxed{1}$
  5   6
$+$ 3   4
   9   0

$7 + 5 = \boxed{1}\,\boxed{2}$

tens ones
$\boxed{1}$
  3   7
$+$ 2   5
   6   2

$6 + 9 = \boxed{1}\,\boxed{5}$

tens ones
$\boxed{1}$
  1   6
$+$ 4   9
   6   5

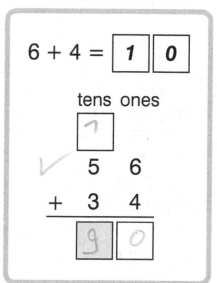

$7 + 8 = \boxed{1}\,\boxed{5}$

tens ones
$\boxed{1}$
  2   7
$+$ 3   8
   6   5

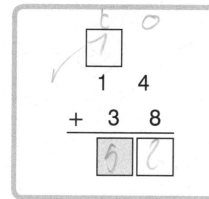

$\boxed{1}$
  1   4
$+$ 3   8
   5   2

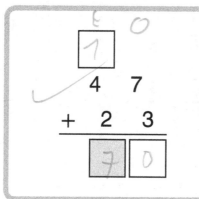

$\boxed{1}$
  4   7
$+$ 2   3
   7   0

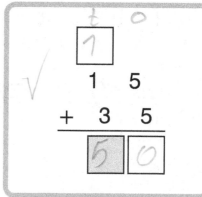

$\boxed{1}$
  1   5
$+$ 3   5
   5   0

NS2-42 The Standard Algorithm for Addition *(continued)*

☐ Add the ones first.
☐ Then add the tens to find the total.

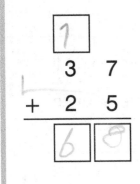

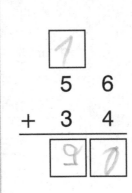

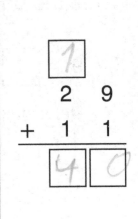

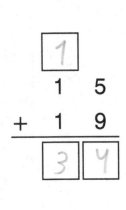

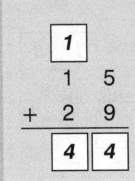

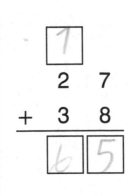

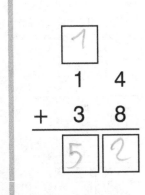

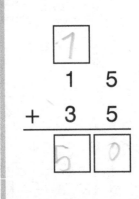

NS2-42 The Standard Algorithm for Addition *(continued)*

☐ Regroup only when you need to.

☐ Add using the standard algorithm.

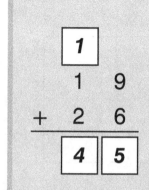

	1	
	1	9
+	2	6
	4	**5**

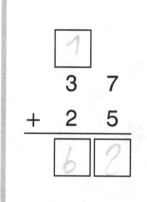

	0	
	2	5
+	3	3
	5	**8**

	1	
	3	7
+	2	5
	6	2

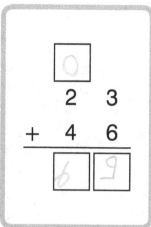

	0	
	2	3
+	4	6
	6	9

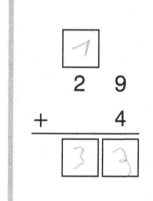

	1	
	2	9
+		4
	3	3

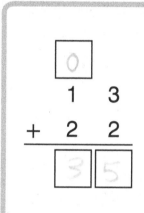

	0	
	1	3
+	2	2
	3	5

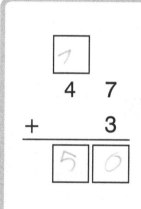

	1	
	4	7
+		3
	5	0

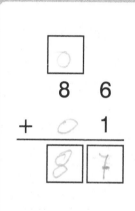

	0	
	8	6
+	0	1
	8	7

Lee added the tens before the ones.

☐ Circle the answers she got wrong.

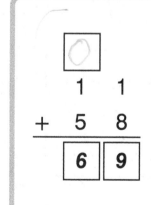

	0	
	1	1
+	5	8
	6	**9**

	1	
	1	7
+	2	7
	3	**4**

	1	
	2	6
+	2	6
	4	**2**

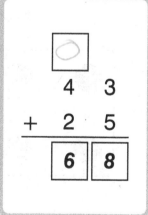

	0	
	4	3
+	2	5
	6	**8**

☐ 29 + 14   37 + 46   48 + 23   55 + 39

NS2-43 **Doubles**

☐ Draw the same number of dots on the other side.
☐ Write a doubles sentence.

10 is double **5**

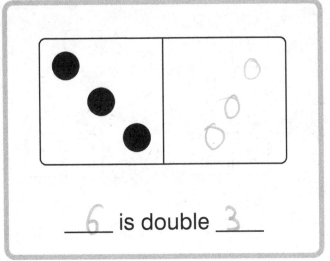

___6___ is double ___3___

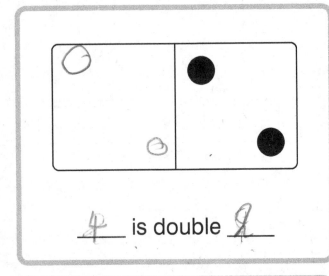

___4___ is double ___8___

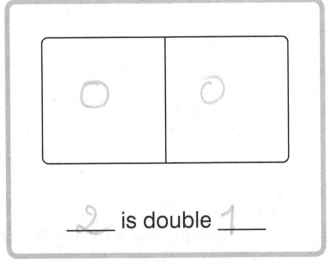

___2___ is double ___1___

___8 is double___

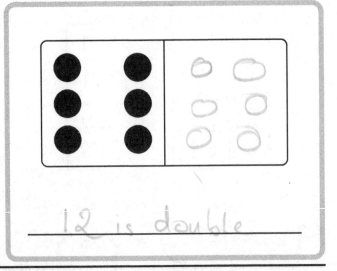

___12 is double___

NS2-44 **Using Doubles to Add**

☐ Double, then add 1.

$4 + 4 = \underline{\textbf{8}}$

so $4 + 5 = \underline{\textbf{9}}$

$3 + 3 = \underline{6}$

so $4 + 3 = \underline{7}$

$7 + 7 = \underline{14}$

so $8 + 7 = \underline{15}$

$8 + 8 = \underline{16}$

so $8 + 9 = \underline{17}$

$6 + 6 = \underline{12}$

so $6 + 7 = \underline{13}$

$5 + 5 = \underline{10}$

so $6 + 5 = \underline{11}$

$\underline{7} + \underline{7} = \underline{14}$

so $7 + 8 = \underline{15}$

$\underline{5} + \underline{5} = \underline{10}$

so $5 + 4 = \underline{9}$

$\underline{5} + \underline{5} = \underline{10}$

so $5 + 6 = \underline{11}$

$\underline{10} + \underline{10} = \underline{20}$

so $10 + 9 = \underline{19}$

Bonus: Find $32 + 33$.

NS2-44 **Using Doubles to Add** (continued)

☐ Double, then subtract 1.

$7 + 7 = \underline{14}$ so $7 + 6 = \underline{13}$	$9 + 9 = \underline{18}$ so $8 + 9 = \underline{17}$
$6 + 6 = \underline{12}$ so $6 + 5 = \underline{11}$	$8 + 8 = \underline{16}$ so $7 + 8 = \underline{15}$
$8 + 8 = \underline{16}$ so $8 + 7 = \underline{15}$	$5 + 5 = \underline{10}$ so $4 + 5 = \underline{9}$
$\underline{10} + \underline{9} = \underline{19}$ so $\quad 9 + 10 = \underline{19}$	$\underline{9} + \underline{9} = \underline{18}$ so $\quad 9 + 8 = \underline{17}$
$\underline{4} + \underline{4} = \underline{8}$ so $\quad 3 + 4 = \underline{7}$	$\underline{8} + \underline{8} = \underline{16}$ so $\quad 7 + 8 = \underline{15}$

Bonus: Find 24 + 23.

NS2-44 **Using Doubles to Add** (continued)

☐ Write how many **more** or **less**.
☐ Find the double.
☐ Add.

4 + 5 is _____1 more than_____ 4 + 4

4 + 4 = __8__ so 4 + 5 = __9__

7 + 9 is _____2 less than_____ 9 + 9

9 + 9 = __18__ so 7 + 9 = 16

6 + 8 is _____2 less than_____ 8 + 8

8 + 8 = __16__ so 6 + 8 = __14__

6 + 7 is _____1 less than_____ 7 + 7

7 + 7 = __14__ so 6 + 7 = __13__

8 + 10 is _____2 less than_____ 10 + 10

10 + 10 = __20__ so 8 + 10 = __18__

7 + 6 is _____

_____ so 7 + 6 = ____

☐ Which two questions have the same answer?
Why did that happen?

NS2-45 Subtraction Strategies

13 − 3 = _____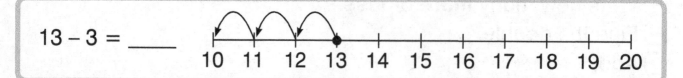

23 − 3 = _____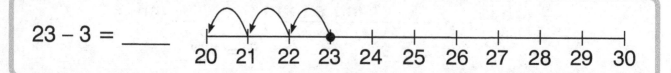

33 − 3 = _____

43 − 3 = _____

73 − 3 = _____

63 − 3 = _____

93 − 3 = _____

53 − 3 = _____

83 − 3 = _____

82 − 2 = _____

67 − 7 = _____

54 − 4 = _____

91 − 1 = _____

85 − 5 = _____

76 − 6 = _____

89 − 9 = _____

50 − 0 = _____

28 − 8 = _____

74 − 4 = _____

68 − 8 = _____

41 − 1 = _____

NS2-45 **Subtraction Strategies** (continued)

◻ Write how many more or less.
◻ Subtract.

74 – 3 is _____**1 more than**_____ 73 – 3

73 – 3 = **70** so 74 – 3 = **71**

83 – 5 is _____**2 less than**_____ 85 – 5

85 – 5 = ____ so 83 – 5 = ____

74 – 6 is _____ 76 – 6

76 – 6 = ____ so 74 – 6 = ____

57 – 6 is _____ 56 – 6

56 – 6 = ____ so 57 – 6 = ____

46 – 9 is _____ 49 – 9

49 – 9 = ____ so 46 – 9 = ____

◻ Solve 75 – 8 in two ways.
◻ **Bonus:** Solve 75 – 8 in a third way.

NS2-46 More Subtraction Strategies

☐ Subtract by adding.

What is 80 – 56?

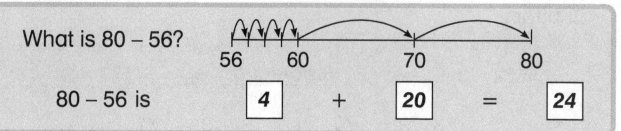

80 – 56 is ⟦ **4** ⟧ + ⟦ **20** ⟧ = ⟦ **24** ⟧

What is 90 – 72?

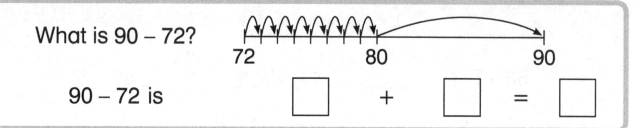

90 – 72 is ⟦ ⟧ + ⟦ ⟧ = ⟦ ⟧

What is 83 – 40?

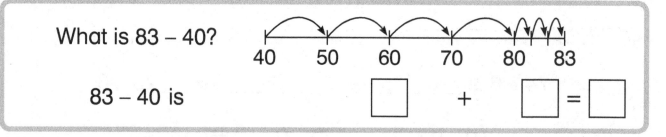

83 – 40 is ⟦ ⟧ + ⟦ ⟧ = ⟦ ⟧

What is 90 – 57?

57 ⌣ 60 ⌣ 90

90 – 57 is ⟦ ⟧ + ⟦ ⟧ = ⟦ ⟧

What is 75 – 40?

40 ⌣ 70 ⌣ 75

75 – 40 is ⟦ ⟧ + ⟦ ⟧ = ⟦ ⟧

What is 30 – 3?

3 ⌣ 10 ⌣ 30

30 – 3 is ⟦ ⟧ + ⟦ ⟧ = ⟦ ⟧

What is 64 – 20?

20 ⌣ 60 ⌣ 64

64 – 20 is ⟦ ⟧ + ⟦ ⟧ = ⟦ ⟧

What is 77 – 40?

40 ⌣ 70 ⌣ 77

77 – 40 is ⟦ ⟧ + ⟦ ⟧ = ⟦ ⟧

What is 80 – 16?

16 ⌣ 20 ⌣ 80

80 – 16 is ⟦ ⟧ + ⟦ ⟧ = ⟦ ⟧

NS2-47 Subtracting Using Tens and Ones

☐ Use ones blocks and tens blocks to subtract.
☐ Colour blocks to show the second number.
What number do the **white** blocks show?

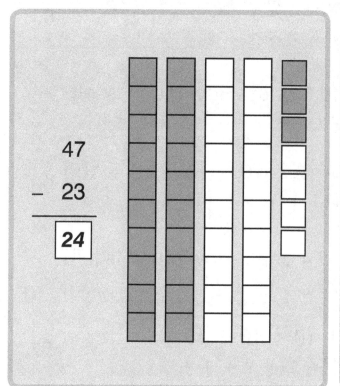

47
− 23
24

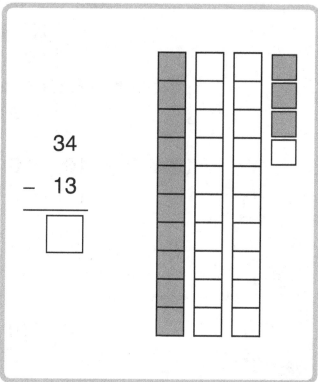

34
− 13
☐

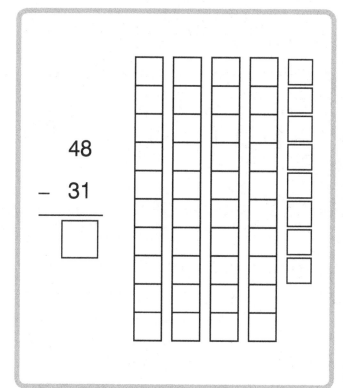

48
− 31
☐

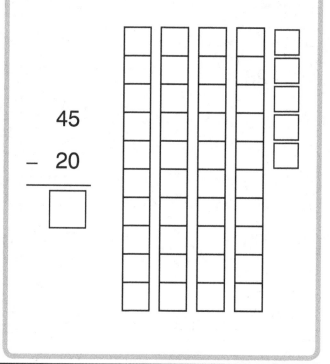

45
− 20
☐

NS2-47 **Subtracting Using Tens and Ones** (continued)

☐ Cross out the correct number of 10s and 1s.
☐ Subtract.

87
− 63
24

X̶ + X̶ + X̶ + X̶ + X̶ + X̶ + 10 + 10
+ X̶ + X̶ + X̶ + 1 + 1 + 1 + 1   ⟩ 87

Cross out 6 tens and 3 ones. How much is left?

96
− 34
☐

10 + 10 + 10 + 10 + 10 + 10 + 10 + 10 + 10
+ 1 + 1 + 1 + 1 + 1 + 1   ⟩ 96

Cross out 3 tens and 4 ones. How much is left?

57
− 31
☐

10 + 10 + 10 + 10 + 10
+ 1 + 1 + 1 + 1 + 1 + 1 + 1   ⟩ 57

Cross out ____ tens and ____ one. How much is left?

28
− 11
☐

10 + 10
+ 1 + 1 + 1 + 1 + 1 + 1 + 1 + 1   ⟩ 28

65
− 34
☐

10 + 10 + 10 + 10 + 10 + 10
+ 1 + 1 + 1 + 1 + 1

34
+ ☐
☐

Check by adding your answer. Do you get 65?

NS2-47 Subtracting Using Tens and Ones *(continued)*

☐ Subtract.

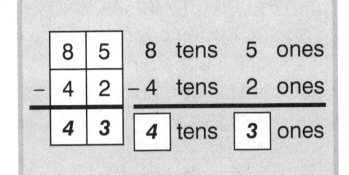

		8 tens	5 ones
8	5		
−4	2	−4 tens	2 ones
4	**3**	**4** tens	**3** ones

		6 tens	7 ones
6	7		
−2	5	−2 tens	5 ones
		☐ tens	☐ ones

		9 tens	7 ones
9	7		
−2	1	−2 tens	1 ones
		☐ tens	☐ ones

		6 tens	3 ones
6	3		
−4	2	−4 tens	2 ones
		☐ tens	☐ ones

☐ Subtract, then check your answer by adding.

tens	ones		check
6	9		5 3
−5	3		+

tens	ones		check
8	5		3 1
−3	1		+

tens	ones		check
7	8		
−3	7		+

tens	ones		check
6	9		
−2	4		+

NS2-48 **Regrouping for Subtraction**

To find 45 – 28, Miki draws tens and ones blocks for 45. She tries to colour 28.

Miki can only colour 25, so she trades a tens block for 10 ones blocks. Now Miki can colour 28.

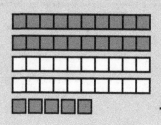

$$45 - 28 = 17$$
There are 17 left.

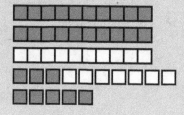

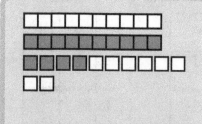

_____

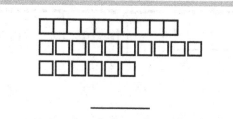

_____

☐ Write the subtraction sentence for the model.

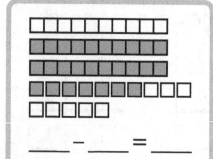

__32__ – __14__ = __18__

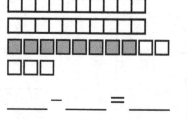

____ – ____ = ____

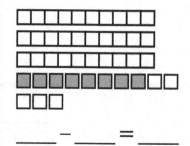

____ – ____ = ____

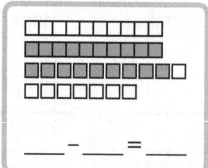

____ – ____ = ____

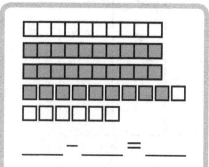

____ – ____ = ____

NS2-48 **Regrouping for Subtraction** (continued)

⬜ Show Miki's trade in a tens and ones chart.

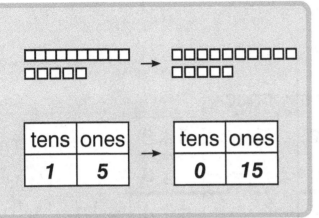

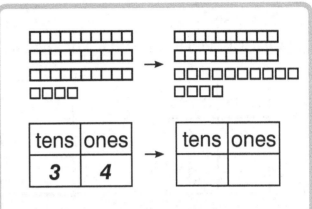

⬜ Show Miki's subtraction using a tens and ones chart.

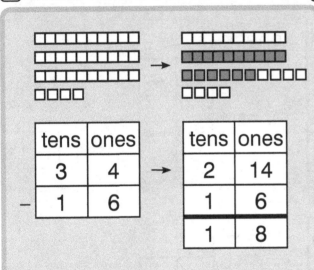

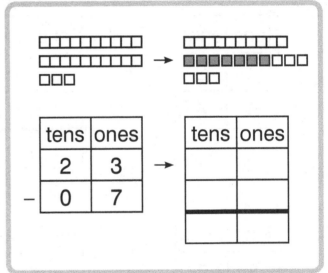

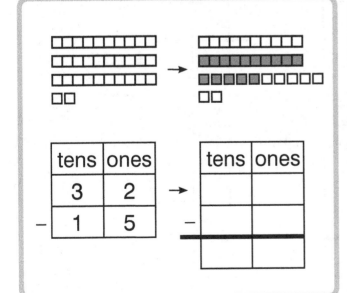

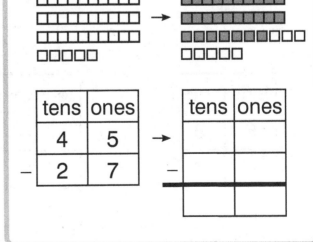

NS2-48 **Regrouping for Subtraction** *(continued)*

☐ Trade a ten for 10 ones.
☐ Subtract.
☐ Check your answer by adding.

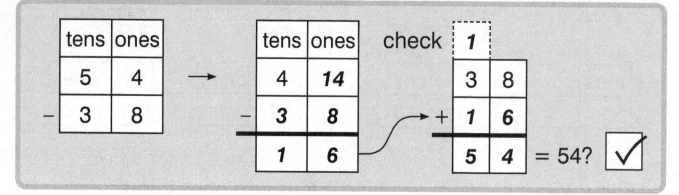

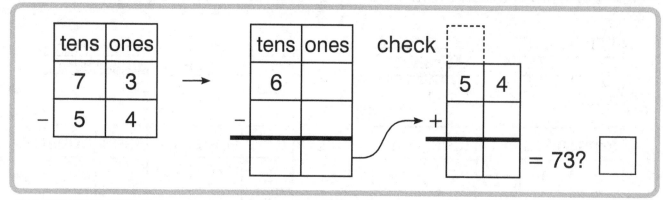

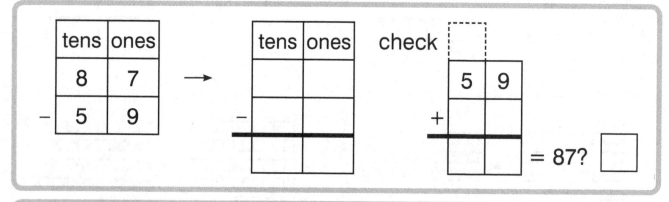

NS2-49 The Standard Algorithm for Subtraction

☐ Take 1 ten from the tens and add 10 ones to the ones.
☐ Use standard notation.

50 = __5__ tens + __0__ ones   **4 10**
   = __4__ tens + __10__ ones | 5̸ | 0 |

73 = __7__ tens + __3__ ones
   = ____ tens + ____ ones | 7 | 3 |

85 = ____ tens + ____ ones
   = ____ tens + ____ ones | 8 | 5 |

5 11
| 6̸ | 1̸ | | 7 | 7 | | 8 | 6 | | 4 | 2 |

| 3 | 9 | | 1 | 6 | | 2 | 3 | | 7 | 1 |

| 4 | 5 | | 5 | 4 | | 3 | 0 | | 3 | 2 |

| 6 | 8 | | 5 | 5 | | 2 | 9 | | 9 | 0 |

NS2-49 The Standard Algorithm for Subtraction *(cont'd)*

☐ Subtract using the standard algorithm.

	6	15
	~~7~~	~~5~~
−	5	7
	1	**8**

	8	3
−	5	6

	5	4
−	3	9

	4	6
−	2	7

	9	2
−	8	7

	8	1
−	5	5

	5	3
−	2	9

	6	0
−	3	6

	9	1
−	7	2

	9	6
−	2	9

	8	7
−	3	8

	8	0
−	5	7

📓 Check your answers by adding.

NS2-49 The Standard Algorithm for Subtraction *(cont'd)*

☐ Decide if you need to regroup. Subtract.

	4	8
−	2	5

	4	7
−	1	9

	4	9
−	1	7

	5	3
−	4	8

	5	8
−	4	3

	6	7
−	3	3

	5	8
−	2	6

	7	0
−	3	7

	8	1
−	6	1

	9	8
−	2	7

	8	5
−	3	6

	9	0
−	4	8

☐ Check your answers by adding.

NS2-49 The Standard Algorithm for Subtraction *(cont'd)*

◻ Subtract in two ways.

standard	by adding
``` 8 5 - 3 3 ```	33 ⌣ 40 ⌣ 80 ⌣ 85 ◻ + ◻ + ◻ = ◻
``` 7 2 - 5 6 ```	56 ⌣ 60 ⌣ 70 ⌣ 72 ◻ + ◻ + ◻ = ◻
``` 9 6 - 4 9 ```	49 ⌣ 50 ⌣ 90 ⌣ 96 ◻ + ◻ + ◻ = ◻
``` 6 8 - 4 3 ```	43 ⌣ 50 ⌣ 60 ⌣ 68 ◻ + ◻ + ◻ = ◻

📓 Subtract by adding to find 72 – 13.

Who is right? Explain what the others did wrong.

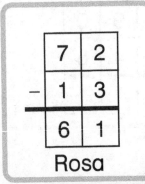

Rosa

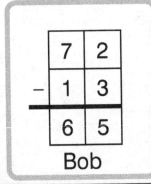

Bob

	12
7	1̸
– 1	3
6	9

Sam

6	12
7̸	2̸
– 1	3
5	9

Lina

NS2-50 Three-Digit Numbers

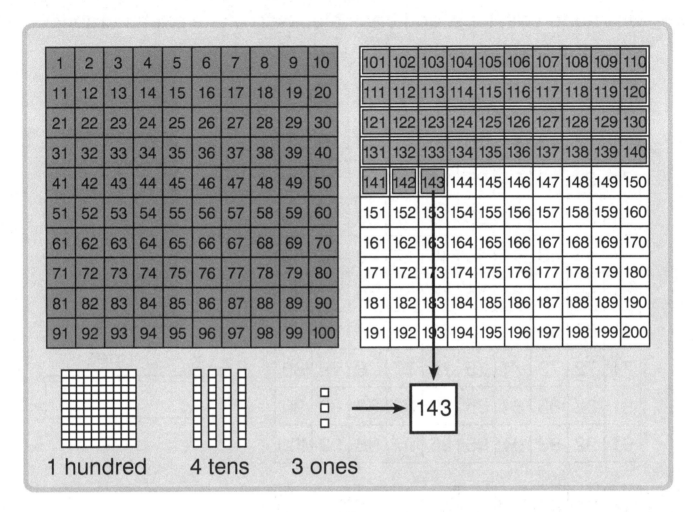

1 hundred　　　4 tens　　　3 ones

What number does each set show?

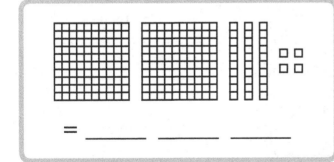

= _____ _____ _____

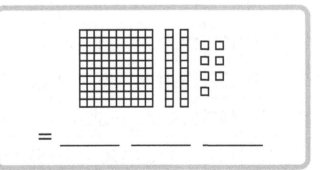

= _____ _____ _____

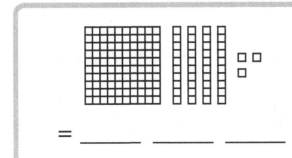

= _____ _____ _____

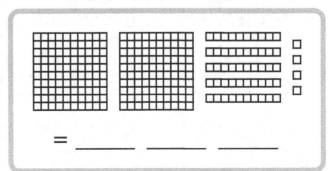

= _____ _____ _____

NS2-50 **Three-Digit Numbers** (continued)

☐ Use hundreds, tens, and ones blocks to make each number.
☐ Write the number you made.

1	2	3	4	5	6	7	8	9	10
11	12	13	14	15	16	17	18	19	20
21	22	23	24	25	26	27	28	29	30
31	32	33	34	35	36	37	38	39	40
41	42	43	44	45	46	47	48	49	50
51	52	53	54	55	56	57	58	59	60
61	62	63	64	65	66	67	68	69	70
71	72	73	74	75	76	77	78	79	80
81	82	83	84	85	86	87	88	89	90
91	92	93	94	95	96	97	98	99	100

101	102	103	104	105	106	107	108	109	110
111	112	113	114	115	116	117	118	119	120
121	122	123	124	125	126	127	128	129	130
131	132	133	134	135	136	137	138	139	140
141	142	143	144	145	146	147	148	149	150
151	152	153	154	155	156	157	158	159	160
161	162	163	164	165	166	167	168	169	170
171	172	173	174	175	176	177	178	179	180
181	182	183	184	185	186	187	188	189	190
191	192	193	194	195	196	197	198	199	200

1 hundred
4 tens
+ 3 ones

☐

14 tens
+ 3 ones

☐

13 tens
+ 13 ones

☐

12 tens
+ 23 ones

☐

NS2-50 Three-Digit Numbers *(continued)*

☐ Add.

4   +   3

= 1 + 1 + 1 + 1   +   1 + 1 + 1   = _____

40   +   30

= 10 + 10 + 10 + 10   +   10 + 10 + 10   = _____

400   +   300

= 100 + 100 + 100 + 100   +   100 + 100 + 100   = _____

2 + 4 = _____

20 + 40 = _____

200 + 400 = _____

3 + 2 = _____

30 + 20 = _____

300 + 200 = _____

1 + 7 = _____

10 + 70 = _____

100 + 700 = _____

5 + 4 = _____

50 + 40 = _____

500 + 400 = _____

1 + 2 + 4 = _____

10 + 20 + 40 = _____

100 + 200 + 400 = _____

2 + 2 + 5 = _____

20 + 20 + 50 = _____

200 + 200 + 500 = _____

Bonus: 60 + 2 + 100 + 4 + 20 + 400 = _____

NS2-51 Skip Counting by Different Numbers

☐ Skip count by ⟨5s⟩, then by ⟨1s⟩.

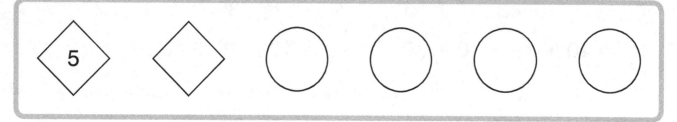

☐ Skip count by 10s, then by ⟨1s⟩.

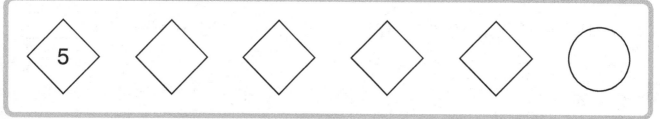

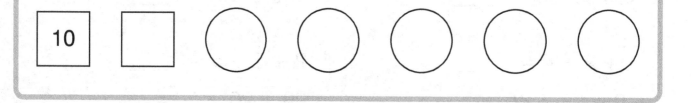

NS2-51 **Skip Counting by Different Numbers** *(continued)*

⬜ Skip count by 10s, then by ◇5s◇.

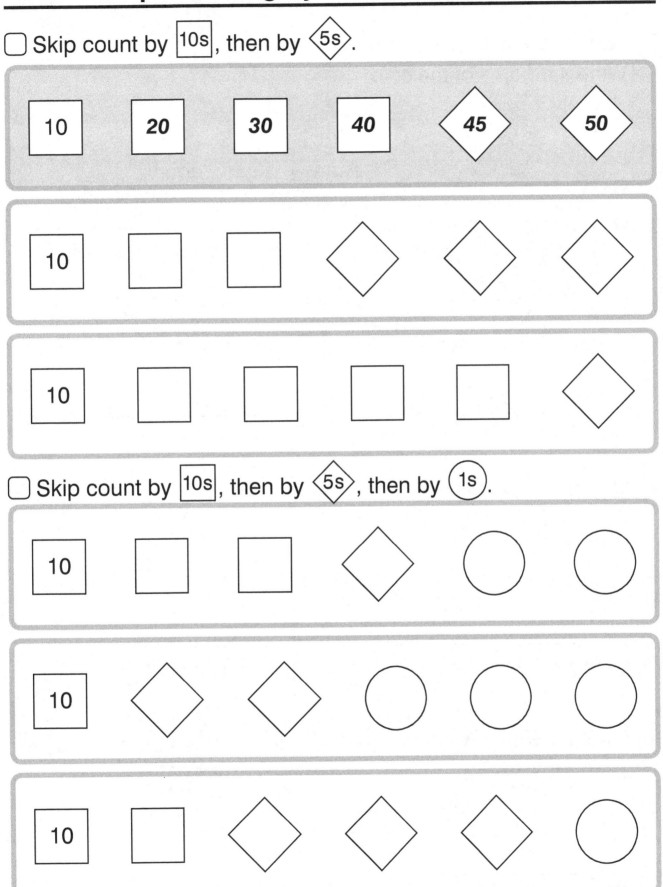

| 10 | 20 | 30 | 40 | 45 | 50 |

10 ▢ ▢ ◇ ◇ ◇

10 ▢ ▢ ▢ ▢ ◇

⬜ Skip count by 10s, then by ◇5s◇, then by ⬤1s.

10 ▢ ▢ ◇ ◯ ◯

10 ◇ ◇ ◯ ◯ ◯

10 ▢ ◇ ◇ ◇ ◯

NS2-52 **Coin Values**

☐ Write the value on the coin.
☐ Write the name of the coin.

| quarter | loonie | dime |
| nickel | ~~penny~~ | toonie |

___*penny*___

_____

_____

_____

_____

_____

NS2-53 Estimating and Counting Money

Does Lisa have enough money?

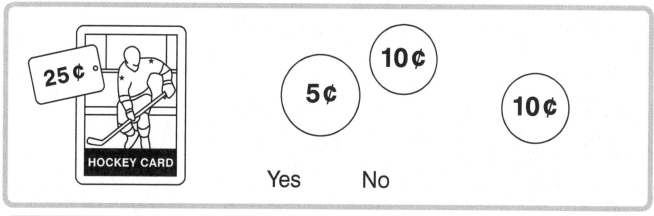

Yes   No

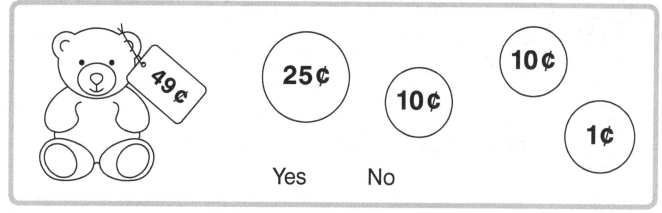

Yes   No

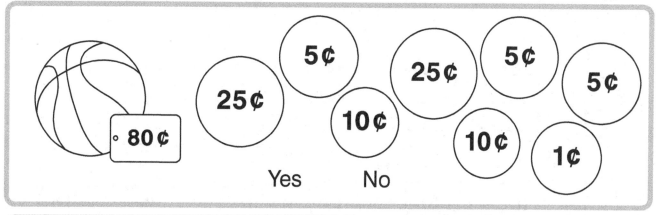

Yes   No

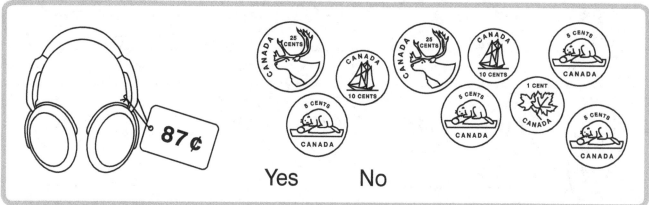

Yes   No

NS2-54 **Adding Money**

☐ Mary adds coins to her bag.
  How much money does she have now?

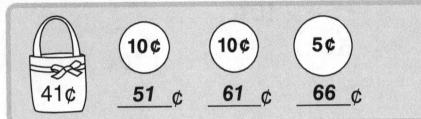

41¢ | 10¢ __51__ ¢ | 10¢ __61__ ¢ | 5¢ __66__ ¢

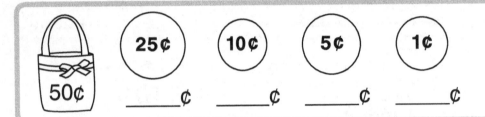

50¢ | 25¢ ___¢ | 10¢ ___¢ | 5¢ ___¢ | 1¢ ___¢

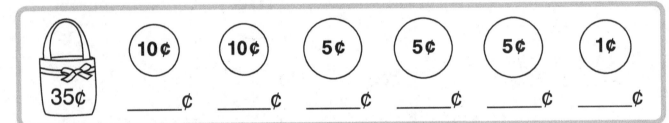

35¢ | 10¢ ___¢ | 10¢ ___¢ | 5¢ ___¢ | 5¢ ___¢ | 5¢ ___¢ | 1¢ ___¢

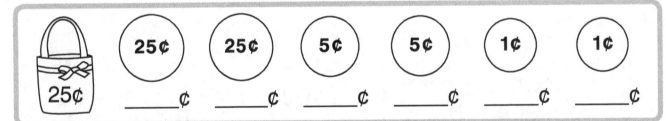

25¢ | 25¢ ___¢ | 25¢ ___¢ | 5¢ ___¢ | 5¢ ___¢ | 1¢ ___¢ | 1¢ ___¢

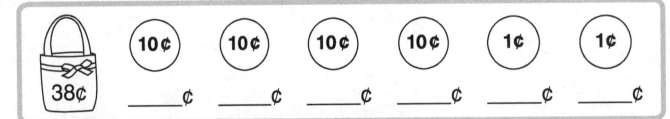

38¢ | 10¢ ___¢ | 10¢ ___¢ | 10¢ ___¢ | 10¢ ___¢ | 1¢ ___¢ | 1¢ ___¢

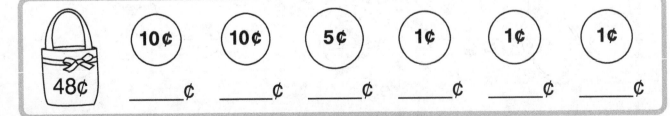

48¢ | 10¢ ___¢ | 10¢ ___¢ | 5¢ ___¢ | 1¢ ___¢ | 1¢ ___¢ | 1¢ ___¢

NS2-54 **Adding Money** *(continued)*

☐ Bilal adds coins to his bag.
How much money does he have now?

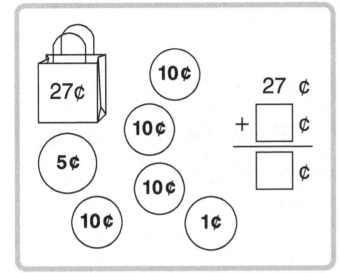

$$27 \ ¢$$
$$+ \ \square \ ¢$$
$$\overline{\quad} \ \square \ ¢$$

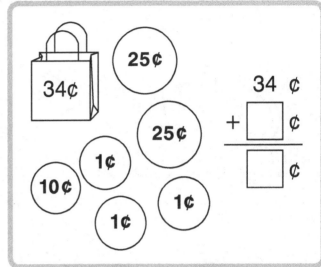

$$34 \ ¢$$
$$+ \ \square \ ¢$$
$$\overline{\quad} \ \square \ ¢$$

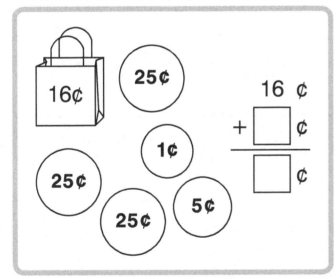

$$16 \ ¢$$
$$+ \ \square \ ¢$$
$$\overline{\quad} \ \square \ ¢$$

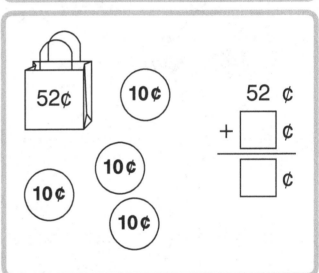

$$52 \ ¢$$
$$+ \ \square \ ¢$$
$$\overline{\quad} \ \square \ ¢$$

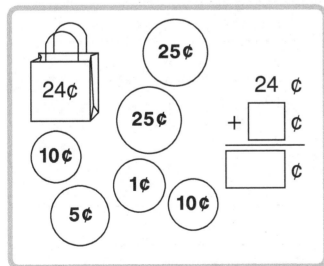

$$24 \ ¢$$
$$+ \ \square \ ¢$$
$$\overline{\quad} \ \square \ ¢$$

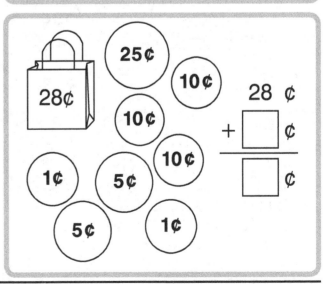

$$28 \ ¢$$
$$+ \ \square \ ¢$$
$$\overline{\quad} \ \square \ ¢$$

NS2-55 Subtracting Money

Lisa pays for stickers.
How much money will she get back?

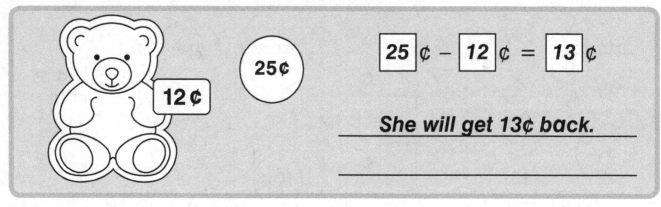

$$25 ¢ - 12 ¢ = 13 ¢$$

She will get 13¢ back.

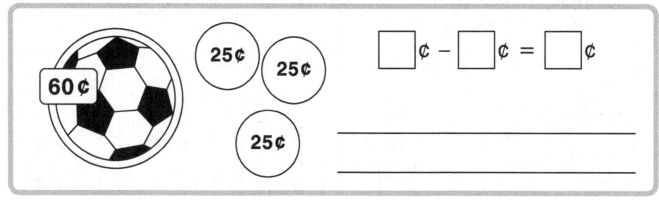

$$\boxed{} ¢ - \boxed{} ¢ = \boxed{} ¢$$

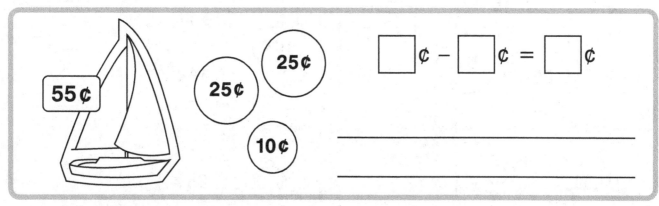

$$\boxed{} ¢ - \boxed{} ¢ = \boxed{} ¢$$

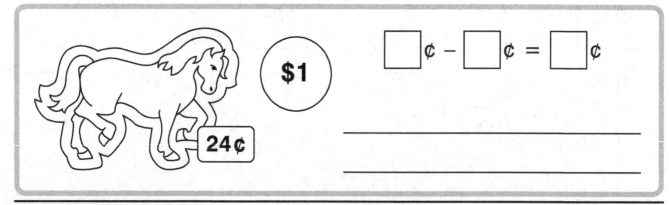

$$\boxed{} ¢ - \boxed{} ¢ = \boxed{} ¢$$

NS2-55 Subtracting Money (continued)

☐ Write an addition or subtraction sentence.
☐ Solve the problem.

Rosa has 17¢.

She finds 3 dimes.

Rosa now has _____¢.

$$\begin{array}{r} 17 \\ + \ 30 \\ \hline 47 \end{array}$$

Miki has 60¢.

She gave her sister a quarter.

Miki has _____¢ left.

Daniel has 2 dimes and 3 nickels.

Ron has 2 quarters.

Ron has _____¢ more than Daniel.

Ahmed has 3 nickels and 7 pennies.

Lina has 2 dimes.

Ahmed and Lina have _____¢ altogether.

NS2-56 **Fractions**

☐ Write half, third, fourth, or fifth.

There are two equal parts.

Each part is a ____half____.

There are **th**ree equal parts.

Each part is a _____.

There are **four** equal parts.

Each part is a _____.

There are **fi**ve equal parts.

Each part is a _____.

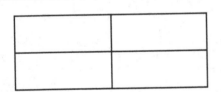

Each part is a _____.

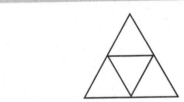

Each part is a _____.

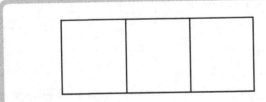

Each part is a _____.

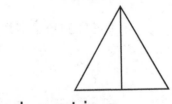

Each part is a _____.

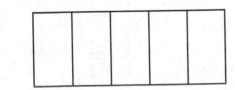

Each part is a _____.

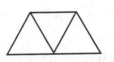

Each part is a _____.

NS2-56 **Fractions** *(continued)*

☐ Colour the fraction.

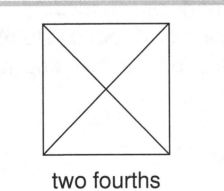
two thirds

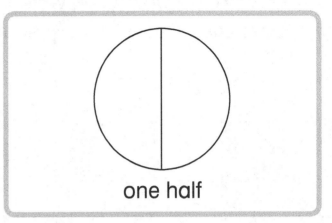
one half

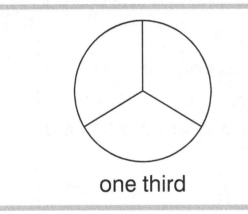
one third

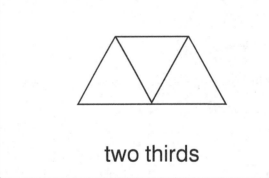
three fifths

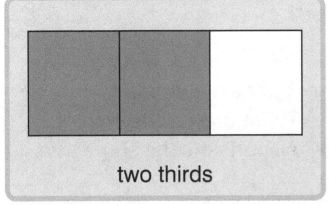
three fourths

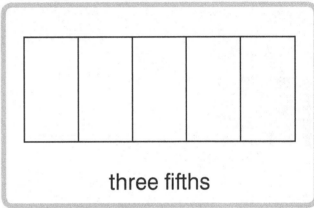
two thirds

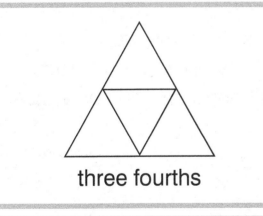
two fourths

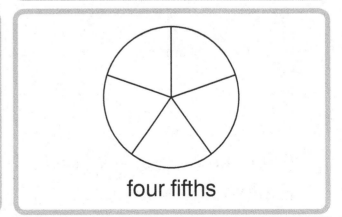
four fifths

NS2-56 Fractions *(continued)*

☐ ✓ what is true and ✗ what is not true.
Does the picture have $\frac{3}{4}$ shaded?

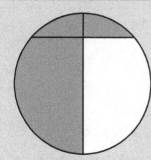

_____ *no* _____

☑ 3 parts are shaded.
☑ There are 4 parts in total.
☒ All parts are the same size.

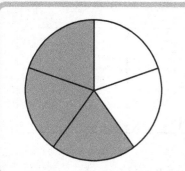

_____

☐ 3 parts are shaded.
☐ There are 4 parts in total.
☐ All parts are the same size.

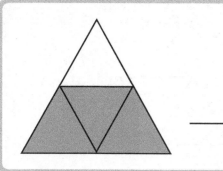

_____

☐ 3 parts are shaded.
☐ There are 4 parts in total.
☐ All parts are the same size.

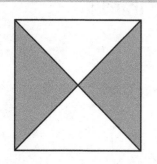

_____

☐ 3 parts are shaded.
☐ There are 4 parts in total.
☐ All parts are the same size.

☐ Does the picture have $\frac{2}{5}$ shaded?
Explain how you know.

NS2-57 Comparing Fractions

☐ Fill the measuring cups the correct amount.
☐ Circle the cup that is more full.
☐ Write **more** or **less**.

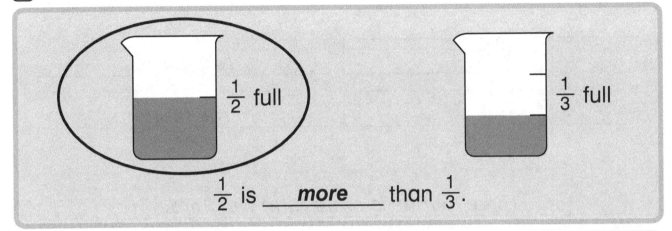

$\frac{1}{2}$ is _____**more**_____ than $\frac{1}{3}$.

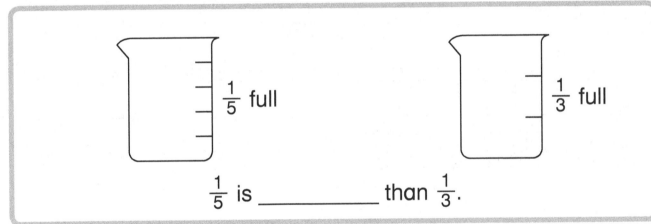

$\frac{1}{5}$ is _____ than $\frac{1}{3}$.

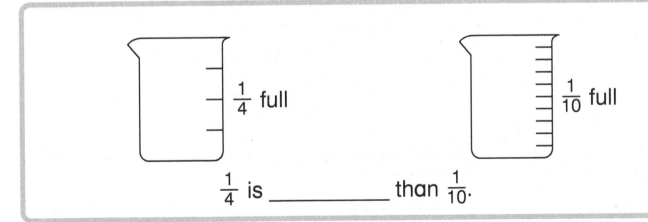

$\frac{1}{4}$ is _____ than $\frac{1}{10}$.

☐ Dividing something into more parts makes each part

_____.
　　smaller / bigger

NS2-57 **Comparing Fractions** (continued)

What fraction does each picture show?
Which fraction is more?

two thirds

three fourths

Three fourths is more than two thirds .

NS2-58 Multiplication

$$2 + 2 + 2 + 2 + 2 \quad = \quad 5 \times 2 \quad = \quad 5 \text{ times } 2$$

☐ Fill in the blanks.

$2 + 2 + 2 + 2 = \underline{\hspace{1cm}} \times 2$

$2 + 2 + 2 = \underline{\hspace{1cm}} \times 2$

$2 + 2 + 2 + 2 + 2 + 2 + 2 + 2 + 2 \quad = \quad \underline{\hspace{1cm}} \times 2$

$3 + 3 + 3 + 3 + 3 + 3 \quad = \quad \underline{\hspace{1cm}} \times 3$

$7 + 7 + 7 + 7 + 7 + 7 \quad = \quad \underline{\hspace{1cm}} \times \underline{\hspace{1cm}}$

$8 + 8 + 8 + 8 + 8 + 8 \quad = \quad \underline{\hspace{1cm}} \times \underline{\hspace{1cm}}$

$12 + 12 + 12 + 12 + 12 + 12 + 12 \quad = \quad \underline{\hspace{1cm}} \times \underline{\hspace{1cm}}$

$100 + 100 + 100 \quad = \quad \underline{\hspace{1cm}} \times \underline{\hspace{1cm}}$

$10 + 10 + 10 + 10 + 10 + 10 + 10 + 10 \quad = \quad \underline{\hspace{1cm}} \times \underline{\hspace{1cm}}$

NS2-58 **Multiplication** *(continued)*

☐ Multiply by counting the dots.

$$
\begin{array}{r}
4 \\
+\ 4 \\
\hline
\end{array}
$$

$2 \times 4 = \boxed{}$

rows →   ↑ in each row

$$
\begin{array}{r}
6 \\
+\ 6 \\
\hline
\end{array}
$$

$2 \times 6 = \boxed{}$

$$
\begin{array}{r}
4 \\
4 \\
+\ 4 \\
\hline
\end{array}
$$

$3 \times 4 = \boxed{}$

$$
\begin{array}{r}
3 \\
3 \\
+\ 3 \\
\hline
\end{array}
$$

$3 \times 3 = \boxed{}$

$$
\begin{array}{r}
7 \\
+\ 7 \\
\hline
\end{array}
$$

$2 \times 7 = \boxed{}$

$$
\begin{array}{r}
3 \\
3 \\
3 \\
+\ 3 \\
\hline
\end{array}
$$

$4 \times 3 = \boxed{}$

☐ Now draw the dots, then multiply.

$$
\begin{array}{r}
2 \\
2 \\
+\ 2 \\
\hline
\end{array}
$$

$3 \times 2 = \boxed{}$

$$
\begin{array}{r}
5 \\
+\ 5 \\
\hline
\end{array}
$$

$2 \times 5 = \boxed{}$

NS2-59 Multiplication by Skip Counting

☐ Keep track as you go along.

| 6 | 9 | 12 | 15 |

$5 \times 3 =$ __3__ + __3__ + __3__ + __3__ + __3__ = | 15 |

☐ ☐ ☐

$4 \times 5 =$ ___ + ___ + ___ + ___ = ☐

☐ ☐ ☐ ☐ ☐

$6 \times 10 =$ ___ + ___ + ___ + ___ + ___ + ___ = ☐

☐ ☐ ☐ ☐ ☐

$6 \times 2 =$ ___ + ___ + ___ + ___ + ___ + ___ = ☐

☐ ☐ ☐ ☐

$5 \times 4 =$ ___ + ___ + ___ + ___ + ___ = ☐

☐ ☐ ☐

$4 \times 3 =$ ___ + ___ + ___ + ___ = ☐

No unauthorized copying

NS2-59 **Multiplication by Skip Counting** *(continued)*

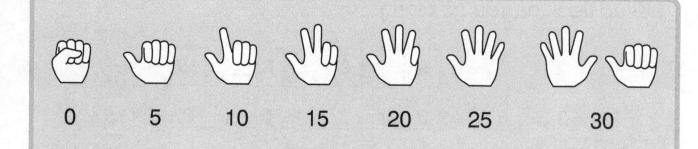

0	5	10	15	20	25		30

☐ Multiply.

3 × 5 = _____	4 × 5 = _____	5 × 5 = _____
1 × 5 = _____	0 × 5 = _____	6 × 5 = _____

☐ Count by 3s.

0   *3*   ___   ___   ___   ___   ___

☐ Multiply.

2 × 3 = _____	4 × 3 = _____	1 × 3 = _____
6 × 3 = _____	3 × 3 = _____	0 × 3 = _____

NS2-60 How Many Groups?

☐ Divide the people into groups of 3.

How many groups? _____

How many groups? _____

How many groups? _____

How many groups? _____

How many groups? _____

NS2-60 **How Many Groups?** (continued)

◻ Find how many groups.

How many groups of 2? __4__

How many groups of 5? _____

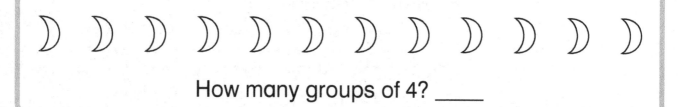

How many groups of 4? _____

How many groups of 2? _____

How many groups of 4? _____

How many groups of 2? _____

UNIT 6

Patterns and Algebra 2

PA2-6 Growing Patterns

6  8 | 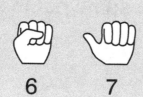 6 7 8 | 6 + 2 = 8
8 is 2 more than 6.

☐ Write the number you add in the circles.

8  9 | 6  9 | 7  9 | 3  7

2 (+) 4 | 11 ◯ 13 | 10 ◯ 16 | 5 ◯ 8

4 ◯ 7 | 12 ◯ 18 | 10 ◯ 17 | 10 ◯ 20

2 ◯ 4 ◯ 6 | 5 ◯ 10 ◯ 15

15 ◯ 16 ◯ 17 | 8 ◯ 10 ◯ 12

8 ◯ 10 ◯ 12

 says the next number is 14. How does she know?

_____

PA2-6 **Growing Patterns** (continued)

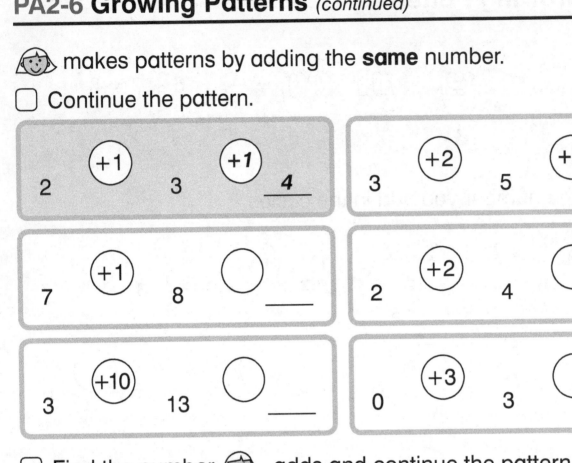

🙂 makes patterns by adding the **same** number.

☐ Continue the pattern.

2 (+1) 3 (+1) __4__

3 (+2) 5 (+2) ____

7 (+1) 8 ○ ____

2 (+2) 4 ○ ____

3 (+10) 13 ○ ____

0 (+3) 3 ○ ____

☐ Find the number 🙂 adds and continue the pattern.

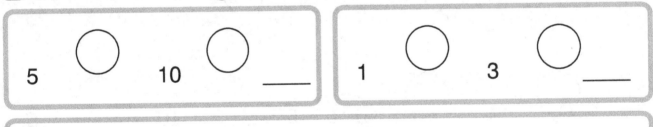

5 ○ 10 ○ ____

1 ○ 3 ○ ____

4 ○ 14 ○ ____ ○ ____ ○ ____ ○ ____

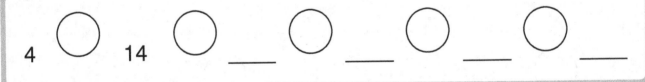

7 ○ 9 ○ ____ ○ ____ ○ ____ ○ ____

20 ○ 25 ○ ____ ○ ____ ○ ____ ○ ____

PA2-7 Shrinking Patterns

 **-3** 8   5

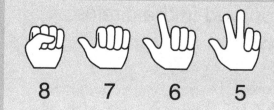 8   7   6   5

$8 - 3 = 5$
5 is 3 less than 8.

☐ Write the number you subtract in the circles.

 **-1**   6   5

4 ◯– 3

5 ◯– 2

6 ◯– 4

7 ◯– 6

8 ◯– 4

12 ◯– 10

12 ◯– 11

16 ◯ 14

19 ◯ 15

18 ◯ 12

17 ◯ 10

7 ◯ 6 ◯ 5

10 ◯ 9 ◯ 8

6 ◯ 4 ◯ 2

13 ◯ 12 ◯ 11

8 ◯ 6 ◯ 4

 says the next number is 2. How does he know?

_____

PA2-8 Describing Patterns

☐ Write the number you add in the circles.
☐ Describe the pattern.

(+2) (+2)

1   3   5

Start at __1__.

Add __2__ each time.

(+) (+)

4   6   8

Start at ____.

Add ____ each time.

(+) (+)

5   6   7

Start at ____.

Add ____ each time.

(+) (+)

10   15   20

Start at ____.

Add ____ each time.

○ ○ ○ ○ ○

10   20   30   40   50   60

Start at ____. Add _____.

○ ○ ○ ○ ○

7   10   13   16   19   22

Start at ____. _____.

○ ○ ○ ○ ○

0   5   10   15   20   25

_____. _____.

PA2-8 **Describing Patterns** (continued)

☐ Write the number you subtract in the circles.
☐ Describe the pattern.

7 (−2) **5** (−2) **3**
Start at __7__.
Subtract __2__ each time.

8 (−) **7** (−) **6**
Start at ____.
Subtract ____ each time.

10 (−) **8** (−) **6**
Start at ____.
Subtract ____ each time.

30 (−) **20** (−) **10**
Start at ____.
Subtract ____ each time.

12 ( ) **10** ( ) **8** ( ) **6** ( ) **4** ( ) **2**
Start at ____. Subtract _____.

18 ( ) **15** ( ) **12** ( ) **9** ( ) **6** ( ) **3**
Start at ____. Subtract _____.

35 ( ) **30** ( ) **25** ( ) **20** ( ) **15** ( ) **10**
Start at ____. _____.

PA2-9 Identifying Patterns

☐ Describe the pattern.

| 1 | 3 | 5 | 7 | 9 |

Start at __1__.

Add __2__ each time.

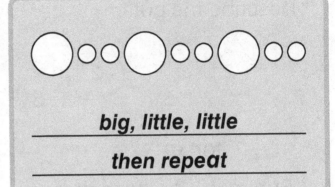

_____ **big, little, little** _____

_____ **then repeat** _____

| 8 | 7 | 6 | 5 | 4 |

Start at ____.

Subtract _____.

| 30 | 40 | 50 | 60 | 70 |

Start at ____.

Add _____.

| 12 | 10 | 8 | 6 | 4 |

_____

_____

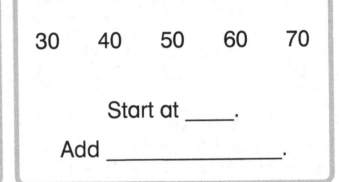

_____

_____

| 5 | 10 | 15 | 20 | 25 |

_____

_____

| 100 | 98 | 96 | 94 |

_____

_____

PA2-10 **Finding Mistakes**

What is the missing room number?

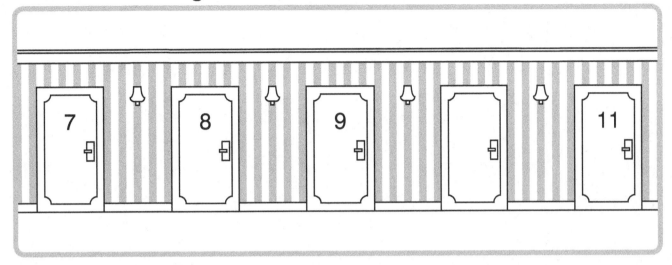

What is the missing house number?

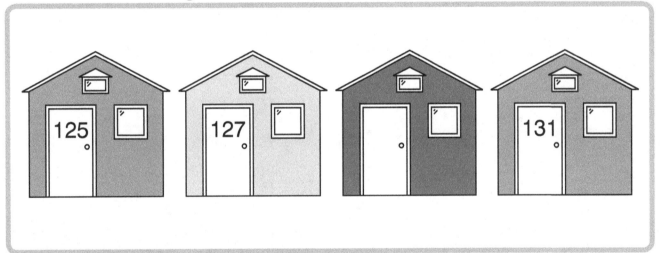

☐ Find the missing book pages.

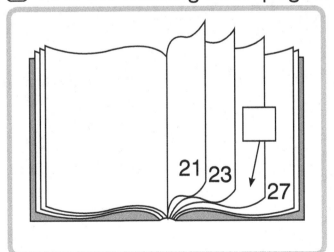

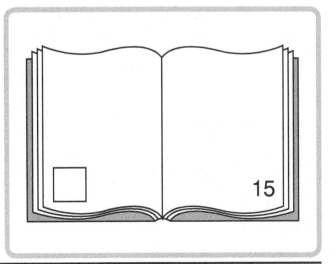

UNIT 7

Measurement 2

ME2-5 **Clock Faces**

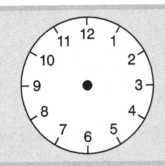

This is a clock face.

Numbers start at 1 and end at 12.

☐ Fill in the missing 3, 6, 9, and 12.

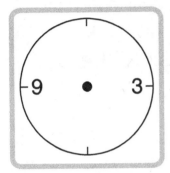 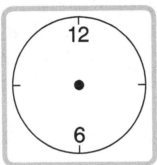 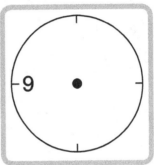 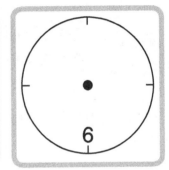

☐ Fill in the missing numbers. Start with 3, 6, 9, and 12.

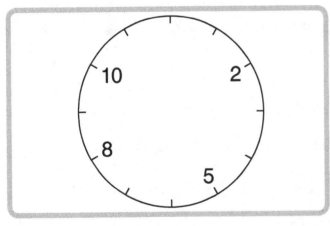 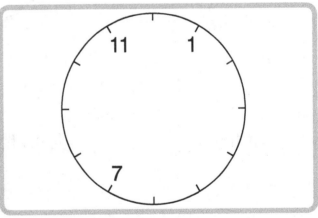

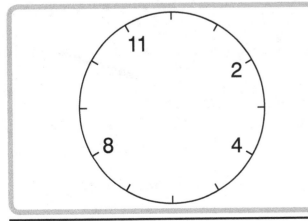 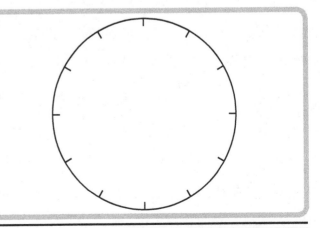

ME2-6 The Hour Hand

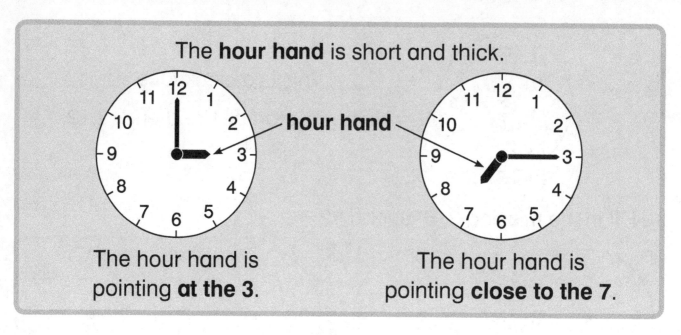

The **hour hand** is short and thick.

hour hand

The hour hand is pointing **at the 3**.

The hour hand is pointing **close to the 7**.

Where is the hour hand pointing?

at the ____

close to the ____

at the ____

close to the ____

at the ____

close to the ____

ME2-6 **The Hour Hand** *(continued)*

☐ Write **before** or **after**.

 It is a little _____**before**_____ 7 o'clock.

 It is a little _____ 1 o'clock.

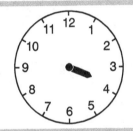 It is a little _____ 4 o'clock.

 It is a little _____ 12 o'clock.

 It is a little _____ 6 o'clock.

 It is a little _____ 11 o'clock.

ME2-6 The Hour Hand *(continued)*

What time is it?

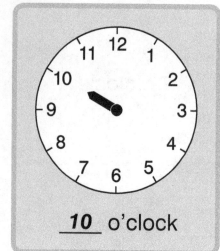

___**10**___ o'clock

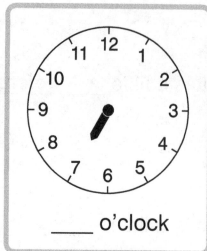

____ o'clock

____ o'clock

a little **after**
____ o'clock

a little **before**
____ o'clock

a little **after**
____ o'clock

a little **before**
____ o'clock

half way between
____ o'clock and
____ o'clock

half way between
____ o'clock and
____ o'clock

No unauthorized copying

ME2-6 **The Hour Hand** *(continued)*

☐ Write the time.

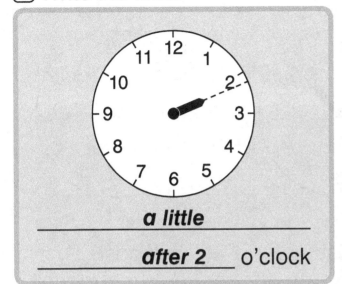

a little
_____

after 2 _____ o'clock

_____ o'clock

_____ o'clock

_____ o'clock

_____

_____

_____

_____

ME2-6 **The Hour Hand** *(continued)*

☐ Write the time.

half past __7__

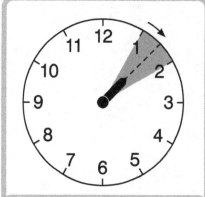

half past ____

half past ____

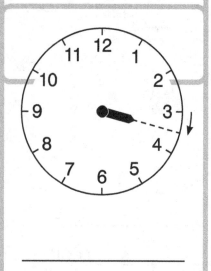

_____

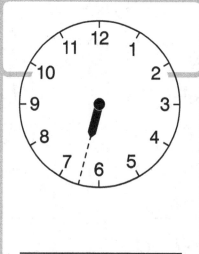

_____

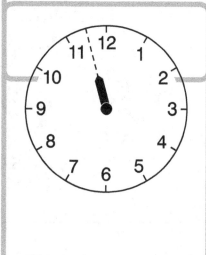

_____

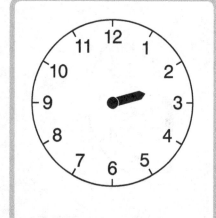

_____

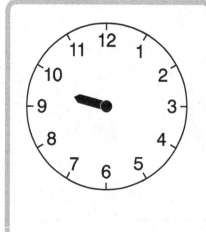

_____

_____

ME2-7 Time to the Hour

It is **9 o'clock** or **9:00**.

☐ Write the time in two ways.

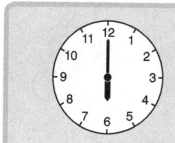

6 o'clock

6 : 00

_____ o'clock

_____ : 00

_____ o'clock

_____ : 00

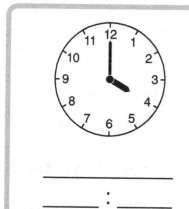

_____

_____ : _____

_____

_____ : _____

_____

_____ : _____

☐ Use a toy clock to show these times.
☐ Circle the two that are the same.

7:00	3 o'clock	5:00
1:00	6 o'clock	1 o'clock

ME2-8 The Minute Hand

How many minutes after 10:00?

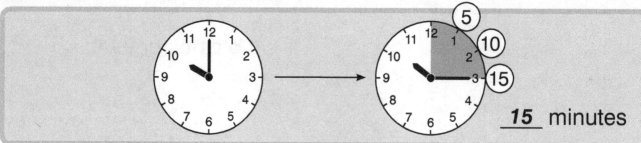

_____ **15** minutes

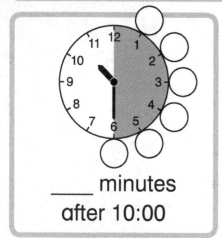

_____ minutes
after 10:00

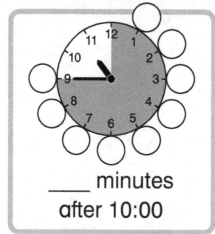

_____ minutes
after 10:00

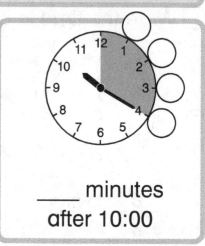

_____ minutes
after 10:00

☐ Write the time.

15 minutes after
7:00 is **7** : **15**

_____ minutes after
_____ is _____ : _____

_____ minutes after
_____ is _____ : _____

_____ minutes after
_____ is _____ : _____

_____ minutes after
_____ is _____ : _____

_____ minutes after
_____ is _____ : _____

ME2-9 Time to the Half Hour

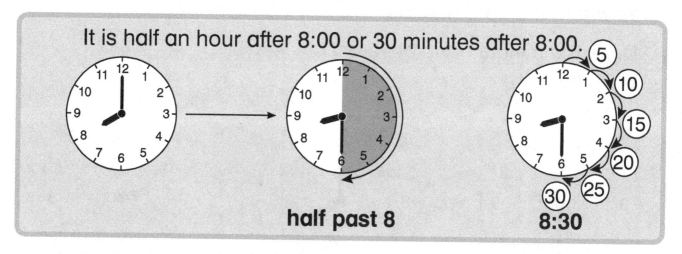

It is half an hour after 8:00 or 30 minutes after 8:00.

half past 8

8:30

☐ Write the time in two ways.

half past _____

_____ : 30

half past _____

_____ : 30

half past _____

_____ : 30

_____

_____ : _____

_____

_____ : _____

_____

_____ : _____

☐ Use a toy clock to show these times.
☐ Circle the two that are the same.

| 12:30 | half past 2 | 4:30 |
| 5:30 | half past 9 | half past 12 |

ME2-9 **Time to the Half Hour** (continued)

Look where the hour hand is.

☐ Draw the minute hand at 12 or 6.
☐ Write the time.

___half past 2___

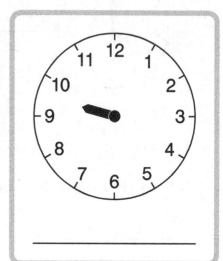

___4 o'clock___

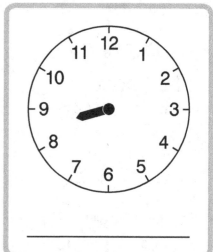

_____

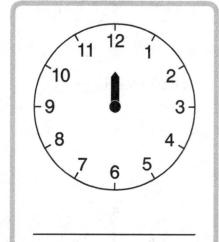

_____

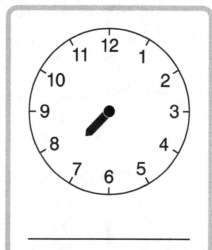

_____

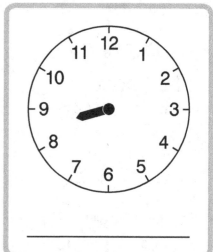

_____

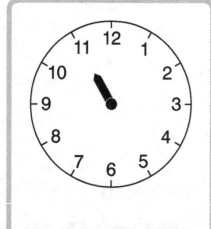

_____

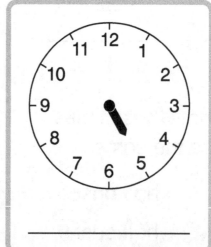

_____

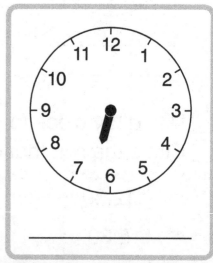

_____

ME2-10 Quarter Past

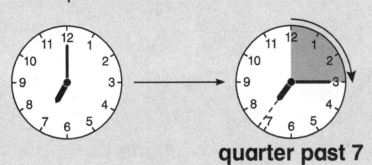

It is a quarter of an hour after 7:00 or 15 minutes after 7:00.

quarter past 7   **7:15**

☐ Write the time in two ways.

quarter past __1__

__1__ : __15__

quarter past ____

____ : ____

quarter past ____

____ : ____

____

____ : ____

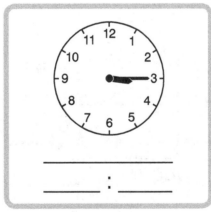

____

____ : ____

____

____ : ____

☐ Use a toy clock to show the times.

☐ Circle the two that are the same.

11:15	quarter past 7	quarter past 2
quarter past 9	8:15	7:15

ME2-11 **Quarter To**

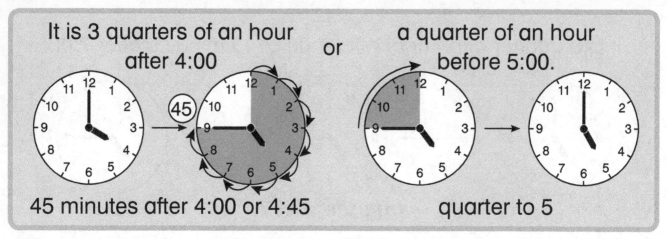

It is 3 quarters of an hour after 4:00 **or** a quarter of an hour before 5:00.

45 minutes after 4:00 or 4:45   quarter to 5

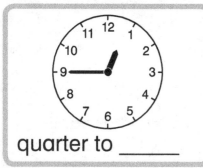

quarter to _____

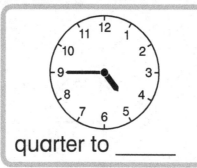

quarter to _____

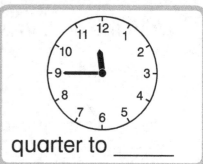

quarter to _____

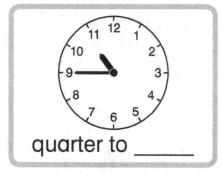

quarter to _____

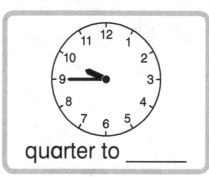

quarter to _____

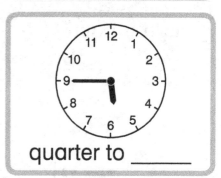

quarter to _____

2:45

quarter to _____

7:45

quarter to _____

8:45

quarter to _____

3:45

quarter to _____

9:45

quarter to _____

6:45

quarter to _____

☐ Circle the times that are the same.

ME2-11 **Quarter To** (continued)

A **quarter** of an hour **before** 4:00 is **quarter to** 4.

A **quarter** of an hour **after** 4:00 is **quarter past** 4.

quarter to 4   4:00   quarter past 4

☐ Write the time.

quarter _**past**_ 7

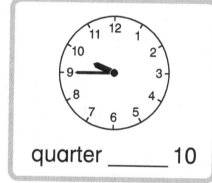

quarter _____ 10

quarter _____ 5

quarter _____

quarter _____

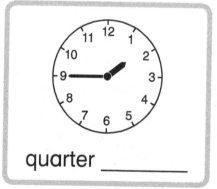

quarter _____

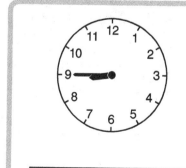

_____

_____

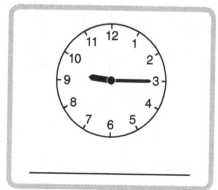

_____

ME2-11 **Quarter To** (continued)

☐ Write the time in two ways.

_____ 7 _____ : _____ 45 _____

quarter to 8

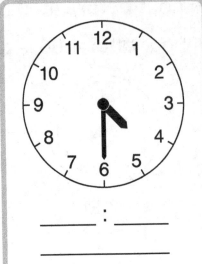

_____ : _____

_____

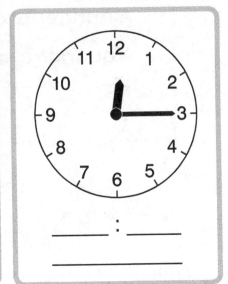

_____ : _____

_____

_____

_____

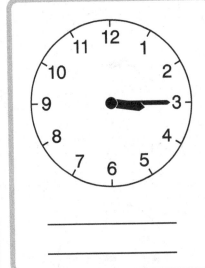

_____

_____

_____

_____

_____

_____

_____

_____

_____

_____

About the Authors

JOHN MIGHTON is a mathematician, author, and playwright. He completed a Ph.D. in mathematics at the University of Toronto and is currently a fellow of the Fields Institute for Mathematical Research. The founder of JUMP Math (www.jumpmath.org), Mighton also gives lectures to student teachers at York University and the Ontario Institute for Studies in Education, and invited talks and training sessions for parents and educators. He is the author of the *JUMP at Home* workbooks and the national bestsellers *The Myth of Ability* and *The End of Ignorance*. He has won the Governor General's Literary Award and the Siminovitch Prize for his plays.

DR. ANNA KLEBANOV received her B.Sc., M.Sc., Ph.D., and teaching certificate from the Technion – Israel Institute of Technology. She is the recipient of three teaching awards for excellence. She began her career at JUMP Math as a curriculum writer in 2007, working with Dr. John Mighton and Dr. Sindi Sabourin on JUMP Math's broad range of publications.

DR. SINDI SABOURIN received her Ph.D. in mathematics from Queen's University, specializing in commutative algebra. She is the recipient of the Governor General's Gold Medal Award from Queen's University and a National Sciences and Research Council Postdoctoral Fellowship. Her career with JUMP Math began in 2003 as a volunteer doing in-class tutoring and one-on-one tutoring, as well as working on answer keys. In 2006, she became a curriculum writer working on JUMP Math's broad range of publications.